The Case of
Nikolai Bukharin

The Case of Nikolai Bukharin
by Ken Coates

Spokesman

First published in Great Britain in 1978 by Spokesman, Bertrand Russell House, Gamble Street, Nottingham, NG7 4ET for the Bertrand Russell Peace Foundation.

Printed in Great Britain by The Russell Press Ltd., Nottingham

Contents

Appendices

For A.M. Larina and Y.N. Larin

Had there been, in full, that "restoration of socialist legality" in the USSR, of which Nikita Khrushchev spoke many times in 1956 and later, this little work would have been completely unnecessary. As things are, unfortunately, it is needed very much, as is the campaign to which it is a contribution.

It is offered, in solidarity, to the widow and the son of the man who has been so profoundly wronged, and not only by his own countrymen.

CHAPTER I

Introduction

ˈThe Bertrand Russell Peace Foundation receives very many letters from political prisoners and their relatives and friends. It is sometimes difficult to do anything useful to help those who write in, since we always lack adequate resources, and sometimes find it hard to fund the necessary research and organise an appropriate response. Often we collaborate with other specialised organisations in order to overcome, to a degree, some of the worst of these disabilities. In one way and another, in spite of the difficulties, we have taken up cases in every continent, in countries belonging to both the main power blocs and throughout the third world.

This aspect of our work stems directly from Bertrand Russell's own active commitment to civil liberties, which goes back to the time of the Dreyfuss case. During the first world war, Russell found himself locked up in Brixton (alongside Litvinov, who was later to become first Soviet ambassador in London, and then Soviet Foreign Secretary). Subsequently Russell, no doubt remembering his own experience, became involved in dozens of campaigns for victims of political repression, from cases like that of Sacco and Vanzetti in the United States to that of the Hungarian communist leader Rakosi, who was, after worldwide protests, given over to the Russian government in exchange for a pile of old flags. By the time Russell established his Foundation he had a vast postbag, and was involved in defending prisoners in a score of countries or more at the same time. He helped secure the release of Ambatielos in Greece, of Heinz Brandt from an East German gaol to which he had been abducted, and of Hugo Blanco from Peru. He campaigned for a large number of Jewish people who had fallen foul of the authorities in

Poland and the USSR. At the same time, he defended Arabs who suffered from the ill-attentions of the Israeli government. All this was complex, and he was often accused of inconsistency even by people he had helped: but the true inconsistency in this matter was not his.

When he died, his mail continued unabated. We still get letters which assume him to be alive and kicking against the pricks. Often, we find ourselves troubled by cases which recur from situations with which he had dealt before us. The threat of execution hanging over ex-premier Bhutto of Pakistan powerfully reminds us of the agitation which was necessary whilst he was imprisoned under Ayub Khan. Ben Bella, for whom Russell made numerous intercessions, is still in confinement, and all efforts to secure his release still fail. Well into 1978, we were making representations, for the third time, on behalf of Hugo Blanco, who had now become a member of his country's parliament, but apparently remained vulnerable to arrest and deportation.

With the fall of Khrushchev, the Soviet authorities paid less and less attention to Russell's views and at the same time, repression of dissidents increased. During the Russell Tribunal on Latin American Repression, which met in Rome, we talked with Pavel Litvinov, then recently deported from the USSR, and Jiri Pelikan, in exile from Czechoslovakia, and as a result launched a worldwide university appeal for selected prisoners in both places, which attracted support from tens of thousands of people in many different countries. For this reason, we became familiar with letters from the Soviet Union, even though some of our own correspondence with Soviet citizens was confiscated by the authorities.

In the late Spring of 1978 we received a letter which was qualitatively different, however. It came from the son of the executed Soviet leader, Nikolai Bukharin. He was seeking the reopening of his father's tragic case, and his letter, which is reported below, raised some very important questions.

As will be argued, the Bukharin case is still topical, and will remain so until the issues it raises can be openly and

honestly discussed in the USSR itself. We take pains below
to show that Bukharin was innocent, although we know
very well that this view is widely shared already. The fact
remains, this innocence is still denied by the ruling party
in the Soviet Union, in spite of massive confirming evidence.
Taking some matters with which Russell himself was directly
involved, we can establish an analogue which is relevant. If,
in the case of the Rosenbergs, who were accused of spying
for the USSR, it could be established beyond doubt that
all the key governmental witnesses were lying, and that
indeed nine-tenths of the evidence presented was plainly
perjured: what should we expect the United States Government to do? We happen to believe that the Rosenbergs were
gravely wronged: but although impressive testimony to this
end has already been presented, it bears no comparison with
the overwhelming and watertight evidence that Bukharin
was similarly, and indeed, in one way, far worse, wronged.
Bukharin's reputation was impugned far more seriously
than was that of the two executed Americans. If, in the
case of Hiss, it were to be admitted by Whittaker Chambers
that he had rigged all the evidence personally, what would
be the reaction? The main witnesses in the Bukharin case all
died because they were executed after "confessing", but
the Government itself has confirmed that their stories were
untrue, by rehabilitating them posthumously, sometimes
with honour.

In spite of some regrettable cases, it is clear that since
Mr Khrushchev spoke of "restoring socialist legality", the
scale of arbitrary injustice has been much reduced in the
USSR. Yet those who fondly hope that socialism will
one day establish a society less unjust in all respects than
capitalism will think that the reluctance of the Soviet
Courts to act on this matter is a powerful and continuing
reproach to all such hopes.

An echo of the past, this case retains contemporary
relevance precisely inasmuch as justice continues to be
withheld. In a sense, the longer this grievance continues, the
more painful it will become.

Cartoon appearing in *Krokodil* accusing Trotsky, Zinoviev
and Kamenev of collaboration with Nazi Germany.

CHAPTER II

An Appeal from Moscow

On 2 March 1938 there opened, in Moscow, the trial of Bukharin, Rykov and others. Twenty-one persons were indicted, and after 11 days all were found guilty. Eighteen were sentenced to be shot, and these were despatched immediately: on 15 March, two days after the conclusion of the proceedings. One was sentenced to 25 years imprisonment, and the remaining two to terms of 15 years. Forty years after this event, there are few anywhere in the world who will admit to believing that this dismal process had anything whatever to do with justice: but the Soviet authorities still refuse to conduct an appropriate reassessment of it. Some of the key participants thus remain under the stigma of absurd official slander: notably Nikolai Ivanovich Bukharin and Alexei Ivanovich Rykov.

At a time when there were millions of victims of repression, perhaps these executions were in one way unremarkable. Statistically, there is still dispute about the size of Stalin's death-roll, but there is not an iota of doubt that within it the extinction of a former Soviet premier and a one-time head of the Communist International would contribute a totally imperceptible additional volume of blood.[1] But constitutionally these judicial murders still weigh heavily on the conscience of Soviet society, for reasons which will be argued later. More, until this shameful episode in Soviet history is faced, it will remain impossible for the peoples of the USSR to recover their own full history, and therefore impossible to recover full rationality, after the wild insanities of the Stalin epoch.

Speaking at the XXII Congress of the Communist Party of the Soviet Union, Nikita Khrushchev said:

"Perhaps we should erect a monument in Moscow to perpetuate the memory of the comrades who fell victim to arbitrary rule."

Whether the monument was forthcoming or not, there were many at that time who hoped that open and truthful discussion about this matter would henceforth be assured. No such thing has happened. Since 1964 there has been positive official recoil from such analysis, and the only truthful home-produced modern histories of Soviet development are among those papers which circulate in samizdat, laboriously copied in manuscript and passed from hand to hand.

One such document was circulated soon after June 1977:

"Early in June 1977, an official of the Central Committee, Klimov, phoned at the apartment of A.M. Larina (N.I. Bukharin's widow) and asked that she get in touch with him. On June 9th, since A.M. Larina was out of Moscow, Yu.N. Larin, her son and son of N.K. Bukharin, called the number indicated by Klimov and asked him hadn't he phoned in connection with the letters sent by Bukharin's son and widow on the eve of the 25th Congress (of the Communist Party of the Soviet Union) to the Congress itself, to the Presidium of the Congress, to the Politburo of the Central Committee of the Communist Party of the Soviet Union, and personally to the General Secretary of the CC, CPSU, L.I. Brezhnev, appealing for Bukharin's rehabilitation. Klimov confirmed that his call was connected with this matter and said the following:

'I have been instructed to inform you that your appeal to have Bukharin reinstated in the Party and restored to full membership in the Academy of Sciences of the USSR cannot be granted since the guilty verdicts pertaining to the criminal offences for which he was tried have not been set aside.'

Yu.N. Larin replied that many of Bukharin's co-defendants have been rehabilitated; for example, Krestinsky, Ikramov, and Khodjayev.

Klimov answered that obviously Larin didn't know that the majority of the accused at the trial had not been rehabilitated. Yu.N. Larin asked, 'Do you really believe that Nikolai Ivanovich (Bukharin) murdered Gorky?' Klimov answered: 'That question falls under the jurisdiction of the courts and the procurator's office.' Yu.N. Larin asked: 'Does that mean that you think I should turn to these bodies?' To this Klimov answered: 'That's your right,' but made it clear he oughtn't do that at the present time. 'You should know how complicated the situation is now.'

A.M. Larina and Yu.N. Larin first appealed for N.I. Bukharin's rehabilitation in 1961. Thus the rejection came 16 years after the first request and a year and a half after the last. (V.I. Lenin's friends, E.D. Stasova and V.A. Karpinsky, having made an analogous appeal in 1965, died and consequently never got an answer.)

Having received the foregoing statement, Yu.N. Larin addressed a petition for Bukharin's rehabilitation to the Chairman of the Supreme Court of the USSR on June 11, 1977."[2]

Whether or not this remarkably obtuse reaction can be explained by a hankering, on the part of some section of the Central Committee of the CPSU, to forgive Stalin, it is tragically plain that Larin and his mother have, since 11 June, 1977, got precisely nowhere in their efforts to secure justice for Bukharin.

This explains why Larin felt it necessary to appeal to Enrico Berlinguer for help, in an extraordinary letter which brings the bygone atmosphere of the late 'thirties menacingly back to life:

"Respected Comrade Berlinguer,

I am writing this letter to you on the eve of the 40th Anniversary of the tragic death of my father, Nikolai Ivanovich Bukharin. At that time I was only two years old and naturally was unable to remember my father. But my mother, who had spent many years in Stalin's prisons and camps, miraculously survived and told me the truth about my father. Later G.M. Krzhizhanovsky, one of V.I. Lenin's closest friends, and Old Bolsheviks, who had lived through the terror and who had known Nikolai Ivanovich in one circumstance or another, told me about him. In addition I read many Bolshevik books (which are banned in our country even today and have been preserved only by chance by certain Old Bolsheviks) including books by Nikolai Ivanovich himself and the works of foreign researchers. The information which I obtained in this way helped me to fully appreciate the character and the social and political activity of my father. I understood the enormity of Stalin's crimes, the extent to which he had falsified the history of the Party, the absurdity and stupidity of the accusations levelled against my father at the Plenum of the Central Committtee of February/March 1937 and the trial of the so-called "Right-Trotskyist Bloc". However, on the basis of these absurd charges (espionage, treason, sabotage and murder), my father was expelled from the Central Committee and from the Party and condemned to death.

Beginning in 1961 my mother A.M. Larina and then I myself persistently raised with the highest Party-State organs of the country the question of the withdrawal of the monstrous allegations against N.I. Bukharin and his restoration to Party membership. This question was also raised with the Party leadership by the most senior of the Old Bolsheviks led by the former secretary of the Central Committee of the Party, E.D. Stasova. They died some time ago without receiving an answer and it was only last summer (1977) that we at last received some response in the form of a telephone call. An official of the Commission of Party Control of the Central Committee of the CPSU informed us by telephone that the accusations made at the trial of Bukharin had not been withdrawn as the process of examining the documents relating to the trial had not been completed; the question of the restoration of his Party membership could not, therefore, yet be resolved. This means that 40 years after the execution of my father we have received an answer, which, in effect, confirms the monstrous charges of Stalin. My approach to the Courts (the Supreme Court of the USSR) has been fruitless: the simple truth is they don't answer me.

In a country where the greater part of the population has been brought up on the mendacious 'Short Course' there are many who still consider my father as a traitor and a hireling-of-Hitler although in reality the truth is that he was an outstanding fighter against fascism and in his last years he devoted all his energies to the exposure of fascism and to warnings against the growing fascist threat.

Leaving home for the last time for the Plenum of February/March 1937 (from which he never returned) my father said to my mother 'don't become embittered: there are sad errors in history. I want my son to grow up as a Bolshevik'. He looked on the events which had occurred as tragic but transient; he believed in the ultimate victory of the forces of socialism.

I am not a member of the Party but for my father the word 'Bolshevik' undoubtedly means a fighter for social justice. And we are unable to obtain such justice in our country for a man whom Lenin before his death called 'the favourite of the whole Party'. For my mother, who lived through the horrors of Stalin's camps, who knew many of Lenin's comrades-in-arms, representatives of the old Bolshevik Party − people about whom she preserves in her memory the happiest recollections and of whom she always speaks with tenderness and love − life in such a situation is becoming more and more intolerable. It is inconceivable that people who still carry on their shoulders the burden of Stalin's crimes and have not cast it into the dustbin of history can fight for high ideals.

I am approaching you, Comrade Berlinguer, not only because you are the leader of the largest communist party of western Europe and have thrown off this burden but also because N.I. Bukharin was a Communist-Internationalist, an active member of the International Workers' Movement. He was known to Communists of many countries: they always recalled him with warmth. Some of them are still living and are working in the ranks of the Italian Communist Party. I particularly have in mind Comrade Umberto Terracini.

I am approaching you to ask you to participate in the campaign for the rehabilitation of my father, in whatever form seems to you to be most appropriate.

Not long before his death Nikolai Ivanovich wrote a letter 'to the future generation of leaders of the Party' in which he appealed to them 'to unravel the monstrous tangle of crimes'. My mother learnt the text of this letter by heart in the dark days and after her re-habilitation she passed it on to the Central Committee of the Party. This letter ended with the words:

'Know Comrades that on the banner which you will carry in your victorious march towards communism there is a drop of my blood.'

Yours sincerely,
Yu.Larin (Bukharin)   12.3.78"

The Russell Foundation, having received this message, circulated it in many countries for endorsement, and secured a very wide response. This will be discussed more fully before we conclude: but meantime, since the Soviet authorities insist that Bukharin's innocence is not yet established, we must examine what has happened to the evidence upon which he was convicted.

FOOTNOTES

1. According to Roy Medvedev "Between 1936 and 1938 Stalin broke all records for political terror. The proscriptions of Cor-nelius Sulla killed several thousand Romans. Tens of thousands perished in the reigns of tyrannical emperors like Tiberius, Caligula, and Nero. The cruelest of all the inquisitors, Tomás de Torquemada, is said to have burned 10,220 living people and 6,860 pictures of absent or dead heretics, and sentenced 97,321 people to such punishment as life imprisonment, confiscation of property, and wearing the garment of shame called *sanbenito*. The *oprichnina* of Ivan the Terrible killed some tens of thou-sands; at its height ten to twenty people were killed daily in Moscow. In the Jacobin terror, according to the calculations of an American historian, 17,000 people were sent to the guillotine by revolutionary tribunals. Approximately the same number were condemned without a trial or died in prison. Exactly how many 'suspects' were imprisoned by the Jacobins is not known; the best estimate is 70,000. In nineteenth-century Russia several dozen were executed for political reasons and several hundred, or at most several thousand, 'politicals' died in prison and exile.
    The scale of the Stalinist terror was inmeasurably greater. In 1936-39, on the most cautious estimates, four to five million people were subjected to repression for political reasons. At least four to five hundred thousand of them − above all the high officials − were summarily shot; the rest were given long terms

of confinement. In 1937-38 there were days when up to a thousand people were shot in Moscow alone. These were not streams, these were rivers of blood, the blood of honest Soviet people. The simple truth must be stated: not one of the tyrants and despots of the past persecuted and destroyed so many of his compatriots." *(Let History Judge,* p.239).

2. This document was published in the American Socialist newspaper, *In These Times,* November 16-22, 1977, p.13.

A view of spectators at the trial.

CHAPTER III

The Accusations

The indictment in the case of N.I. Bukharin and others is an
horrendous document, and the whole matter has frequently
been discussed in the Western literature of Soviet affairs.*
These discussions, however, have tended to pay especial
attention to the argument which took place in the Trial
itself, and have generally taken as obvious the falsity of the
great majority of the specific charges. Since this is a matter
which the Control Commission of the Central Committee
of the CPSU now disputes, it is necessary to concentrate
upon the original indictment, in order to show that it is
completely incompatible with a variety of statements and
actions made by subsequent Soviet Government officials
themselves. Accordingly, we shall page up the accusations
alongside our commentary, which, for convenience of
reading, will be set in a different typeface. It should hastily
be added the refutation will be in no way complete, com-
piled as it is by one who is no specialist in the field, without
access to many materials in the case, working at a distance
and with only a general knowledge of recent Soviet politics.
If the indictment cracks under such inexpert scrutiny, this
in itself is a material testimony to its absurdity.

---

*In conveniently accessible form, notably in Robert Conquest:
The Great Terror, Penguin 1971, A.B. Ulam: *Stalin,* Allen Lane
1973, Stephen Cohen: *Bukharin and the Bolshevik Revolution,*
Wildwood House 1974, George Katkov: *The Trial of Bukharin,*
Batsford 1969. These books are only an introductory group which
lead into a vast and complex literature.

Bukharin and Trotsky shown as a two-headed monster labelled "The Right-Trotskyist Monstrosity". The hand holding them back bears the label "Gestapo".

INDICTMENT

in the case of N. I. BUKHARIN, A. I. RYKOV, G. G. YAGODA,
N. N. KRESTINSKY, K. G. RAKOVSKY, A. P. ROSENGOLTZ,
V. I. IVANOV, M. A. CHERNOV, G. F. GRINKO, I. A. ZELENSKY,
S. A. BESSONOV, A. IKRAMOV, F. KHODJAYEV, V. F. SHAR-
ANGOVICH, P. T. ZUBAREV, P. P. BULANOV, L. G. LE-
VIN, D. D. PLETNEV, I. N. KAZAKOV, V. A. MAXIMOV-
✱ DIKOVSKY and P. P. KRYUCHKOV, accused of having on
the instructions of the intelligence services of foreign states hostile
to the Soviet Union formed a conspiratorial group named the "bloc
of Rights and Trotskyites" with the object of espionage on behalf
of foreign states, wrecking, diversionist and terrorist activities,
undermining the military power of the U.S.S.R., provoking a
military attack by these states on the U.S.S.R., dismembering the
U.S.S.R. and severing from it the Ukraine, Byelorussia, the
Central Asiatic Republics, Georgia, Armenia, Azerbaijan and the
Maritime Region of the Far East for the benefit of the aforementioned foreign states, and lastly, with the object of overthrowing
the Socialist social and state system existing in the U.S.S.R. and
of restoring capitalism, of restoring the power of the bourgeoisie.
    The investigation instituted by the organs of the People's Com-
missariat of Internal Affairs has established that on the instructions of the intelligence services of foreign states hostile to the
U.S.S.R. the accused in the present case organized a conspiratorial
group named the "bloc of Rights and Trotskyites," the object of
which was to overthrow the Socialist social and state system existing
in the U.S.S.R., to restore capitalism and the power of the bourgeoisie in the U.S.S.R., to dismember the U.S.S.R. and to sever

---

✱ Of those listed in this indictment, the following have been
reported to be completely "rehabilitated": N.N. Krestinsky,
V.I. Ivanov, M.A. Chernov, G.F. Grinko, I.A. Zelensky,
A. Ikramov, F. Khodjayev and P.P. Kryuchkov. (C.f. R.A.
Medvedev: *Let History Judge,* Spokesman, 1976; and
Bukharin's Last Two Years, New Left Review 109; Robert
Conquest: *The Great Terror,* Penguin, p.690). Peter Yakir,
the son of the General Yakir to whom reference is made
below, states in his samizdat letter *Stalin: a Plea for a
Criminal Investigation* that seventeen of the twentytwo
(sic) accused in the Bukharin Trial were rehabilitated, but
he does not cite dates or references, as does Medvedev.
(See *Survey,* 70/71, 1969, p.266).

from it for the benefit of the aforementioned states the Ukraine, Byelorussia, the Central Asiatic Republics, Georgia, Armenia, Azerbaijan and the Maritime Region.

The investigation has established that the "bloc of Rights and Trotskyites" united within its ranks underground anti-Soviet groups of Trotskyites, Rights, Zinovievites, Mensheviks, Socialist-Revolutionaries and bourgeois nationalists of the Ukraine, Byelorussia, Georgia, Armenia, Azerbaijan and the Central Asiatic Republics, which is corroborated by the materials not only of the present investigation, but also by the materials of the trials which have taken place in various parts of the U.S.S.R., and, in particular, the trial of the group of military conspirators—TUKHACHEVSKY   *
and others—who were convicted by a Special Session of the Supreme Court of the U.S.S.R. on June 11, 1937, and of the trial of the Georgian bourgeois nationalist group of MDIVANI, OKUDJAVA and others, who were convicted by the Supreme Court of the Georgian Soviet Socialist Republic on July 9, 1937.

* Speaking at the 22nd Congress of the CPSU, on 27 October 1961, N.S. Krushchev said:

"After the 20th Congress, which condemned the personality cult, the anti-party group tried hard to prevent further exposures. Molotov said that great causes included something bad and something good. He tried to justify the actions taken in the period of the personality cult and foretold that such actions were possible, that their repetition in the future was possible. That was the line of the anti-party factionist group. This was not just a fallacy. It was a deliberate, criminal, adventurist position. They wanted to push the party, the country, from the Leninist path, wanted to revert to the policy and methods of leadership of the period of the personality cult.

But they miscalculated. The central committee, our entire party, the entire Soviet people, gave a resolute rebuff to the anti-party group, exposed and routed the factionists.

It was with a feeling of pain that many prominent party leaders and statesmen who innocently perished were remembered here.

Among the victims of reprisals were such eminent military leaders as Tukhachevsky, Yakir, Uborevich, Kork, Yegorov, Eideman and others. They were army-men of merit, especially Tukhachevsky, Yakir and Uborevich. They were prominent soldiers. Blucher and other well-known military leaders were victimised later.

A rather curious report leaked out in the foreign press to the effect that Hitler, in preparing the attack on our country planted a forged document through his intelligence service stating that Comrades Yakir, Tukhachevsky and others were agents of the German General Staff. This supposedly secret "document" had fallen into the hands of Czechoslovakia's President Benes, who, evidently guided by good intentions, had forwarded it to Stalin. Yakir, Tukhachevsky and other comrades were arrested and then destroyed.

Many excellent commanders and political workers in the Red Army were destroyed. There are comrades among the delegates here — I don't want to give their names so as not to cause them pain — who have spent many years in prison. They were "persuaded", persuaded in certain ways, that they were German, British or some other spies. And some of them "confessed". Even when they were told that the charges of espionage against them had been withdrawn, they themselves insisted on their earlier despositions as they felt that it would be better to abide by their false statements in order to have done with the torture, to die the quicker.

That is the meaning of the personality cult! That is the meaning of the actions of Molotov and others who wanted to revive the pernicious methods of the personality cult period! It is to that that the anti-party group wanted to turn back the party, and that is precisely why the struggle against them was so bitter and hard. Everyone has understood the meaning of all this.

I was well acquainted with Comrade Yakir. I also knew Tukhachevsky — but not so well as Yakir. This year, during a conference in Alma Ata, I was approached by his son, who works in Kazakhstan. He asked me about his father. What could I tell him?

When we investigated this case in the presidium of the central committee and were told that neither Tukhachesvsky nor Yakir nor Uborevich had perpetrated any crimes against the party or the state, we asked Molotov, Kaganovich and Voroshilov: "Are you in favour of rehabilitating them?"

"Yes, we are in favour", they replied.

"But you yourselves executed these people", we said with indignation. "When were you acting in good faith — then or now?"

They did not reply to this question. And they won't. You have heard what they wrote in letters to Stalin. What, then, cay you say?

In his speech at the congress Comrade Shelepin told you how these finest representatives of the Communist Party in the Red Army were destroyed. He quoted Comrade Yakir's letter to Stalin and read out the resolutions on that letter. It should be said that Yakir had been in good standing with Stalin at one time.

I can add that before his execution Yakir exclaimed: "Long live the party, long live Stalin!"

He trusted the party; he trusted Stalin so much that he could not even think that this act of lawlessness was being committed knowingly. He believed that enemies had penetrated the organs of the NKVD.

When Stalin was told how Yakir bore himself at the execution, Stalin cursed him."*

*(Reply to discussion on The Report of the Programme of the CPSU, October 18 1961. *Soviet News* Booklet No.81, pp.113-4).

Lacking all support within the U.S.S.R., the members of the "bloc of Rights and Trotskyites" in their struggle against the Socialist social and state system existing in the U.S.S.R. and for seizing power placed all their hopes exclusively upon the armed assistance of foreign aggressors, who promised the conspirators this assistance on the condition that the U.S.S.R. was to be dismembered and that the Ukraine, the Maritime Region, Byelorussia, the Central Asiatic Republics, Georgia, Armenia and Azerbaijan were to be severed from the U.S.S.R.

This agreement between the "bloc of Rights and Trotskyites" and the representatives of the aforementioned foreign states was facilitated by the fact that many of the leading participants of this conspiracy had long been agents of foreign intelligence services and had for many years carried on espionage activities on behalf of these intelligence services.

This applies first of all to one of the inspirers of the conspiracy, enemy of the people TROTSKY. His connection with the Gestapo was exhaustively proved at the trials of the Trotskyite-Zinovievite Terrorist Centre in August 1936, and of the Anti-Soviet Trotskyite Centre in January 1937.   *

However, the materials in the possession of the investigating authorities in the present case establish that the connections between enemy of the people TROTSKY and the German political police and the intelligence services of other countries were established at a much earlier date. The investigation has definitely established that TROTSKY has been connected with the German intelligence service since 1921, and with the British Intelligence Service since 1926.

As far as the accused in the present case are concerned, a considerable number of them, on their own confession, have been espionage agents of foreign intelligence services for a long period of time.   **

Thus, the accused N. N. KRESTINSKY, on the direct instructions of enemy of the people TROTSKY, entered into treasonable connections with the German intelligence service in 1921.

---

*   When various Western public figures, including H.G. Wells, invited the prosecution at the postwar Nuremburg Trials of Nazi War Criminals to seek corroboration of these "proofs" their invitation was ignored. In all the voluminous Nazi archives which were captured by the Allies, no such "proof" has been discovered.

**   But N.N. Krestinsky has been rehabilitated. Maisky wrote warmly of him in *Isvestia* (27 September 1963), and he is praised in the *Historical Encyclopaedia*. (See Medvedev, *Let History Judge*, p.181).

The accused A. P. ROSENGOLTZ, one of the leaders of the Trotskyite underground organization, began his espionage work for the German General Staff in 1923, and for the British Intelligence Service in 1926.

The accused K. G. RAKOVSKY, one of L. Trotsky's most intimate and particularly trusted men, has been an agent of the British Intelligence Service since 1924, and of the Japanese intelligence service since 1934.

The accused M. A. CHERNOV began his espionage work on behalf of Germany in 1928, when he established connections with the German intelligence service on the initiative and with the assistance of the notorious émigré Menshevik DAN. *

The accused V. F. SHARANGOVICH was enlisted by the Polish intelligence service and was sent on espionage work to the U.S.S.R. in 1921. **

The accused G. F. GRINKO became a spy of the German and Polish intelligence services in 1932. ***

The leaders of the "bloc of Rights and Trotskyites," including RYKOV, BUKHARIN and others accused in the present case, were fully informed of the espionage connections of their accomplices and did everything to encourage the expansion of these espionage connections.

All this sufficiently explains why these gentlemen, being in the service of foreign intelligence services, so readily agreed to the dismemberment of the U.S.S.R. and to the severance of whole regions and republics from it for the benefit of foreign states.

Agreement between the "bloc of Rights and Trotskyites" and foreign intelligence services was also facilitated by the fact that several of the conspirators accused in the present case had been provocateurs and agents of the tsarist secret police.

Having wormed their way into responsible posts in the Soviet state, these provocateurs, however, never ceased to fear the exposure of the crimes they had committed against the working class, against the cause of Socialism. Constantly in fear of exposure, these participants in the conspiracy saw their only hope of safety in the overthrow of the Soviet power, in the destruction of the Soviet system and in the restoration of the power of the landlords and capitalists, in whose interests they had sold themselves to the tsarist secret police, and under whose rule alone they could feel safe.

---

* Chernov, too, has been rehabilitated.

** All the Polish Communists who were executed without trial on similar accusations have been rehabilitated.

*** Grinko has been rehabilitated.

*   Thus, the accused I. A. ZELENSKY had been an agent of the
Samara Gendarme Administration since 1911. From that time
onwards ZELENSKY, under the pseudonyms of "Ochkasty"
and "Salaf," systematically informed the Gendarme Administration about the activities of the Samara Bolshevik organization, for which he received a regular monthly monetary remu-
neration.

The accused IVANOV began his provocateur activities in
1911, when he was enlisted for this purpose by the Tula Secret
Police and became an agent of the secret police under the pseudo-
** nym of "Samarin."

The accused ZUBAREV was enlisted by the tsarist police in
1908 and worked for them under the pseudonyms of "Vasily,"
"Palin," and "Prokhor."

As the investigation has established, for the purpose of achieving their criminal object of overthrowing the Soviet government,
of seizing power and restoring capitalism in the U.S.S.R., the
conspirators, on the direct instructions of the foreign intelligence
services, carried on extensive espionage work on behalf of these
intelligence services, organized and carried on wrecking and diversion activities with the object of bringing about the defeat of
the U.S.S.R. in the forthcoming attack upon the U.S.S.R. by
the fascist aggressors, did their utmost to provoke the accelera-
tion of this attack of the fascist aggressors, and also organized and
carried out a number of terrorist acts against the leaders of the
Party and the government and prominent Soviet public men.

I. ESPIONAGE AGAINST THE SOVIET STATE AND
TREASON TO THE COUNTRY

The investigation has established that the majority of the
leaders of the "bloc of Rights and Trotskyites" accused in the present
case carried on their criminal activities on the direct instructions of
TROTSKY and in accordance with plans which were widely conceived and elaborated by the General Staffs of certain foreign
states.

Agent of the German intelligence service, prominent Trotskyite, the accused KRESTINSKY, while under examination at the
office of the Procurator of the U.S.S.R. on December 2, 1937,
stated:

"I established espionage connections with the Germans
on the direct instructions of TROTSKY, who instructed me to

---

*   Zelensky has been rehabilitated. (See *Let History Judge*,
p.181).

**   Ivanov has been rehabilitated. *(Ibid.)*

start negotiations on this matter with General SEECKT. . . ."

*   (Vol. III, p. 102.)

As regards the circumstances under which connections between the Trotskyite organization and the German intelligence
service were established, the accused KRESTINSKY testified that
in the winter of 1921 he carried on negotiations with General
SEECKT, Commander-in-Chief of the German Reichswehr, with
a view to receiving from the Reichswehr funds for the purpose of
carrying on Trotskyite underground work in exchange for espionage
materials which the Trotskyites were to supply the German intelligence service.

On this matter the accused KRESTINSKY testified as follows:

". . . TROTSKY instructed me on my arrival in Berlin
to start negotiations on this matter with General SEECKT.
This instruction of TROTSKY'S I carried out. . . ."

(Vol. III, p. 14 reverse.)

Dealing with his own treasonable activities and with those
of his accomplices, the accused KRESTINSKY testified as follows:

"We came to an agreement with Generals SEECKT and
HASSE to the effect that we would help the Reichswehr to
create a number of espionage bases on the territory of the
U.S.S.R. by permitting the unhindered entry of spies sent
by the Reichswehr, and that we would supply the Reichswehr
with espionage materials, i.e., to put it plainly, that we
would be German spies. In return for this the Reichswehr un-
dertook to pay us 250,000 marks per annum as a subsidy for
counter-revolutionary Trotskyite work. . . ."

(Vol. III, p. 102.)

"The monetary subsidy was paid in regular instalments
several times a year, mostly in Moscow, but sometimes in
Berlin. . . .
"If for some reason the money was not paid in Moscow,
I received it in Berlin myself directly from SEECKT; and
I used to take it to Moscow myself and hand it to TROTSKY."

(Vol. III, p. 15.)

Another prominent Trotskyite, one of the leaders of the anti-
Soviet Trotskyite underground organization and an active par-

* Not only has Krestinsky, who repudiated his confession in
the subsequent trial until he was prevailed upon to reassert
it, been rehabilitated, but his work has been enthusiastically
revalued in the Soviet press. Yet, as Conquest writes: "To
rehabilitate Krestinsky without rehabilitating Rosengoltz is
to rehabilitate Burke while leaving Hare accused".

ticipant in the conspiracy, the accused ROSENGOLTZ, who is charged with espionage, during the investigation corroborated the fact that TROTSKY had entered into an agreement with the Reichswehr and testified as follows:

"My espionage activities began as far back as 1923, when, on TROTSKY'S instructions, I handed various secret information to the Commander-in-Chief of the Reichswehr, SEECKT, and to the Chief of the German General Staff, HASSE. Subsequently, direct connections with me were established by the —— Ambassador in the U.S.S.R., Mr. N, to whom I periodically gave information of an espionage character. After Mr. N's departure I continued my espionage connections with the new Ambassador, Mr. N." · (Vol. VI, p. 131 reverse.)

After the fascist coup in Germany, the espionage activities of the Trotskyites assumed a still wider and sharply expressed defeatist character.

The accused BESSONOV, who on his own confession took an active part in the secret negotiations between the Trotskyites and the German fascist, mainly military, circles, on the matter of jointly fighting the U.S.S.R., not only personally negotiated for support for the anti-Soviet conspiracy with DAITZ, ROSENBERG'S closest colleague in the foreign affairs department of the fascist party, but was kept informed of the meetings and negotiations between L. TROTSKY and HESS, NIEDERMEIER and Professor HAUSHOFER, with whom L. TROTSKY reached an agreement on the terms mentioned by PYATAKOV at the trial of the Anti-Soviet Trotskyite Centre.

*   The accused BESSONOV testified:

*   Medvedev reports:

"Bessonov's role, both in the organisation of the trial and in the actual 'scenario', was especially significant. For according to the script, it was precisely he who had allegedly acted as a link between the Trotskyists and Zinovievites and the 'Rights', Bukharin, Rykov, and Tomsky. While working in the Soviet trade delegation in Berlin, he had supposedly arranged meetings of oppositionists with Trotsky and his son Sedov, passed on instructions, and so on. It would be hard to condemn Bessonov for playing this role in the trial, for he did not accept it readily or immediately. He was subjected to the most refined forms of torture. He endured 'the conveyor' without sleep for seventeen days, whereas many others did not last more than four or five. He was continually beaten. But, as in many other cases after a long period of initial resistance, once he broke down and signed the false statements Bessonov no longer had the strength for any further resistance, but became an obedient tool in the hands of the trial organisers." *(Bukharin's Last Two Years: New Left Review,* 109, 1978).

". . . As is evident from these terms . . . the main emphasis in the underground work of the Trotskyites was placed on undermining, espionage, diversion and terrorist acts in the U.S.S.R."   (Vol. XI, p. 106.)

The existence of an agreement between L. TROTSKY and the Trotskyite organization in the U.S.S.R., on the one hand, and the fascist circles, on the other, and the carrying on in the U.S.S.R. of undermining defeatist activities on the instructions of the German intelligence service was admitted during the investigation by other accused in the present case.

However, the defeatist activities of the Trotskyite hirelings were not limited merely to connections with German fascism. In conjunction with other participants in the anti-Soviet conspiracy, in conformity with L. TROTSKY'S line, they orientated themselves also on another fascist aggressor—Japan.

The factual side of the treasonable connections of the anti-Soviet conspirators with the Japanese intelligence service is presented in the materials of the investigation in the following way.

As was testified by the accused KRESTINSKY, at a meeting he had with L. TROTSKY in Meran in October 1933, TROTSKY urged the necessity of establishing closer connections with the Japanese intelligence service.

KRESTINSKY conveyed TROTSKY'S instructions to PYATA-KOV and other leaders of the conspiracy, who through the medium of the accused RAKOVSKY and other participants in the conspiracy entered into treasonable connections with representatives of Japan, the latter undertaking to render the conspiracy armed assistance in overthrowing the Soviet government, in exchange for which the conspirators promised to surrender the Soviet Maritime Region to Japan.

As has been established by the investigation, the accused RA-KOVSKY, in view of his departure for Japan in the summer of 1934, received from PYATAKOV instructions to the effect that it was

". . . necessary at the same time to increase activities abroad in the sense of establishing contact with governments hostile to the U.S.S.R. . . . necessary to make efforts to take advantage of the visit to Tokyo and probably —— will take the necessary steps in this direction."   (Vol. IV, p. 194.)

The accused RAKOVSKY carried out this instruction, and while in Tokyo did indeed enter into criminal connections with—— circles.

On this matter the accused RAKOVSKY testified as follows:

"All these circumstances had as their logical and practical consequence the fact that I . . . when I was in Tokyo became a direct spy-agent of ——, being enlisted for this purpose, on the instructions of ——, by Mr. N, a most influential politic-

at figure in capitalist-feudal Japan, and one of her biggest
plutocrats."   (Vol. IV, p. 186.)

The aforementioned accused RAKOVSKY, speaking of the
connections of enemy of the people L. TROTSKY with the British
Intelligence Service, testified as follows:

"I knew that TROTSKY has been an agent of the Intelligence Service since the end of 1926. TROTSKY himself informed me of it."   (Vol. IV, p. 363.)

The groups of bourgeois nationalists which belonged to the
"bloc of Rights and Trotskyites" were also very closely connected
*   with foreign intelligence services.

Thus, the accused GRINKO, who was an agent of the German
and Polish intelligence services, in dealing with the anti-Soviet
activities of the Ukrainian national-fascist organization of which
he was one of the leaders, testified as follows:

". . . In 1930, we in our organization discussed the necessity of coming to an agreement with Poland about obtain-
ing military assistance for an insurrection in the Ukraine
against the Soviet government. As a result of these negotiations
with Poland an agreement was reached and the Polish General Staff increased the quantity of arms and the number of
diversionists and PETLIURA emissaries sent to the Ukraine."
                                                (Vol. IX, p. 18.)

And he said further:

"At the end of 1932 I, in connection with my nationalist
activities, entered into treasonable connections with Mr. N.
We met in my office, where Mr. N used to come to see me on
business concerning a German concession.

"In the latter half of 1933 Mr. N told me plainly that the
German fascists wanted to co-operate with the Ukrainian
nationalists on the Ukrainian question. I expressed to Mr. N
my readiness to co-operate. Subsequently, during 1933 and
1934, I met Mr. N several times, and before his departure
from the U.S.S.R. he put me in touch with Mr. N, with whom
I continued my treasonable connections."

                                    (Vol. IX, p. 286 reverse.)

Another participant in the anti-Soviet conspiracy, and one

---

*   Not much of the foregoing is able to stand Krestinsky's
      rehabilitation. As for what follows immediately, Grinko too
      has been rehabilitated. (See *Let History Judge*, p.181).

of the leaders of the nationalist organization in Uzbekistan, the
✱ accused IKRAMOV, testified as follows:

> "The question constantly arose before us of orientating
> ourselves upon one of the strong European states, which would
> render us direct assistance at the outbreak of the armed
> struggle against the Soviet power. . . ."

(Vol. XII, pp. 59-60.)

> ". . . Some of the members of the counter-revolutionary
> organization were of the opinion that England was the most
> likely country in regard to helping us, as she was a powerful
> country and could render us sufficiently effective assistance
> in the direct armed struggle. . . ."   (Vol. XII, p. 60.)

The accused SHARANGOVICH, agent of the Polish intelligence service and one of the leaders of the anti-Soviet organization of Byelorussian national-fascists, has admitted that this organization pursued its undermining activities not only on the instructions of the Rights and the "bloc of Rights and Trotskyites,"
✱✱ but also on the instructions of the Polish intelligence service.
On this matter the accused SHARANGOVICH testified as
follows:

> "By this time (1933) all differences between the Rights,
> the Trotskyites and the national-fascists had been ironed
> out. We all set ourselves the same task, the task of fighting
> the Soviet government by every possible method, including
> terrorism, diversion and wrecking. The ultimate object of all
> three organizations operating in the territory of the nation-
> al republic was to sever Byelorussia from the Soviet Union
> and to create an 'independent' buffer state, which undoubt-
> edly would have been entirely in the hands of Poland and
> Germany. . . ."   (Vol. XIV, p. 27.)

And he said further:

> "Notwithstanding the fact that the instructions we re-
> ceived came from Moscow, from the centre of the Rights and
> Trotskyites, on the one hand, and from Warsaw, from Polish

✱ Ikramov's rehabilitation should not distract attention
from the fact that his "confession" reflects a certain
contemporary shift in Stalin's foreign policy. This was
pointed up by Trotsky: *Writings* 1937-8, pp.236 *et.seq.*

✱✱ Sharangovich confessed that Goloded and Cherviakov, the
ByeloRussian Communists, were Polish spies. They, however, have been fully rehabilitated. (See *Let History Judge,*
p.180).

——circles, on the other, there was no difference between them, they were exactly the same, and we were carrying them out.''
(Vol. XIV, p. 31.)

The accused RYKOV fully corroborated the existence of treasonable connections between the Rights and fascist Poland in the following testimony:

"...A group of members of the Right organization, in conformity with the instructions of the centre of the Rights and my personal instructions, with the object of achieving our conspiratorial, treasonable plans, established connection with fascist Poland, and with the Polish intelligence service in particular."
(Vol. I, p. 118.)

Speaking further of the plans to sever Byelorussia from the U.S.S.R., the accused RYKOV testified as follows:

"The general formula on which we then agreed was that in the negotiations with the Poles ... we would agree to the severance of the Byelorussian Soviet Republic from the U.S.S.R. and to the formation of an 'independent' Byelorussia as a Polish protectorate. ..."
(Vol. I, p. 119.)

As has been established by the investigation, the whole of the criminal activities of the anti-Soviet group of Rights which belonged to the "bloc of Rights and Trotskyites" proves that the Rights were agents of foreign General Staffs equally with the other participants in this conspiracy.

Some of the Rights directly, and others through the medium of their accomplices, were also connected with the intelligence services of foreign states, on whose assistance alone they counted in their fight against the Soviet government.

The accused BUKHARIN was aware of the negotiations carried on between L. TROTSKY and the German fascists and, like L. TROTSKY, made preparations for the defeat of the U.S.S.R. and for the severance of the Ukraine, Byelorussia, the Maritime Region, Georgia, Armenia, Azerbaijan and the Central Asiatic Republics from the U.S.S.R.

This has been fully admitted by the accused BUKHARIN, who testified as follows:

"At the time TROTSKY was negotiating with the German fascists and promising them territorial concessions, we Rights were already in a bloc with the Trotskyites. RADEK told me that TROTSKY considered that the main chance of the bloc coming into power depended upon the defeat of the U.S.S.R. in a war with Germany and Japan and that he proposed after this defeat to surrender the Ukraine to Germany and the Far East to Japan. RADEK told me this in 1934. ..."
(Vol. V, p. 107.)

On this matter the accused F. KHODJAYEV testified as follows during the investigation:

"BUKHARIN urged that Uzbekistan and Turkmenia should be severed from the U.S.S.R. and should exist as protectorates of Japan and Germany; but it would be impossible to ignore England, and it was therefore necessary to establish connection with the English. The most feasible proposal was a British protectorate, and that is why stress was laid on England." (Vol. XIII, pp. 89-89 reverse.)

The testimony of the accused F. KHODJAYEV is fully corroborated by other materials of the investigation, which fully expose * the defeatist line of the "bloc of Rights and Trotskyites."

Thus, on this point the accused RYKOV testified as follows:

"As for our defeatist position, BUKHARIN fully agreed with it and expressed himself in its favour even more strongly than we did. In particular, it was he who proposed and formulated the idea of opening the front to the Germans in the event of war." (Vol. I, p. 152.)

Characterizing his own attitude towards this question, the accused RYKOV testified as follows:

"Like the other members of the Rights' centre, I was aware of the treasonable negotiations that were being carried on between the representatives of our counter-revolutionary organization and the German fascists, whose assistance we sought. Naturally, this assistance was dependent upon our making concessions to the German fascists, and to this we agreed." (Vol. I, p. 151 reverse.)

Such were the espionage and defeatist activities of the "bloc of Rights and Trotskyites" of these traitors who sold Soviet state secrets to foreign intelligence services, who traded in the freedom of the peoples of the U.S.S.R., in the independence and inviolability of the workers' and peasants' Socialist states.

In pursuit of their criminal designs, the anti-Soviet conspirators, on the direct instructions of foreign fascist intelligence services, organized a wide network of diversionist and wrecking nests in a number of industrial, transport, agricultural and distributing enterprises in various republics, territories and regions of the Soviet Union.

Entering into an agreement with the fascist circles treacherously to open our fronts to the armies of these fascist states in the event of war, the participants in the Right and Trotskyite conspiracy prepared to undermine the material and technical base of the Red Army—the defence industry.

By preparing for a number of destructive and diversionist ac-

* But Khodjayev has been fully rehabilitated.

tivities, the conspirators counted in the event of war on blowing up
and destroying the decisive defence enterprises in our Socialist
fatherland. They also made preparations to wreck troop-trains,
causing great loss of life.

They set themselves the task of paralysing the whole economic
life of the country, of paralysing the food and munition supplies
of the army.

The investigation has established that the conspirators actually carried out a number of diversionist and wrecking acts of
this kind in various branches of national economy.

As has been established by the investigation, that hireling of
foreign intelligence services, enemy of the people TROTSKY, in
a number of his letters and personal instructions to the leading
participants in the anti-Soviet conspiracy in the U.S.S.R., de-
manded the intensification of wrecking and diversionist activities
in the Soviet Union.

The accused KRESTINSKY, a leading participant in the conspiracy, testified that in 1933, in Meran, L. TROTSKY told him
personally that

> "... it would be easier for him, TROTSKY, to negotiate
> with the Germans if he could tell them that really serious
> work was being carried on in the way of diversionist and
> wrecking activities and preparation for terrorism."
> (Vol. III, pp. 54-55.)

The investigation has established that a number of diversionist acts committed in the Far Eastern Territory were planned and
carried out by the participants in this anti-Soviet conspiracy on
the direct instructions of the Japanese intelligence service and
of enemy of the people L. TROTSKY. Thus, on the instructions of
the Japanese intelligence service they organized the wreck of a
military freight train at Volochayevka Station, and the wreck of
train No. 501 on the Khor-Dormidontovka section, in which 21
persons were killed and 45 injured. In conformity with the same
Japanese instructions, acts of diversion were committed in pits
No. 10 and 20 in Suchan.   (Vol. XLV, pp. 1-14.)

Detailed testimony on similar instructions emanating from
L. TROTSKY has been given by the accused ROSENGOLTZ, who
stated the following:

> "In addition to instructions I received from TROTSKY
> through KRESTINSKY and SEDOV to carry on wrecking acti-
> vities in the sphere of foreign trade with the object of ren-
> dering direct assistance to Germany and Japan, the character
> of my wrecking activities was also determined by instructions
> I received from the —— Ambassadors in the U.S.S.R., Mr. N
> and Mr. N, connections with whom played an important part

---

*   It will be remembered that Krestinsky has been rehabilitated.

in this matter, as I had to be guided in my work by their definite instructions.

"After I had established contact with TUKHACHEVSKY and RYKOV, I informed the former through KRESTINSKY, and the latter I myself informed, of TROTSKY'S instructions regarding wrecking activities, and both approved of the work I had done.

"As the result of all this, wrecking activities in foreign trade proceeded mainly along the following three lines: first—economic assistance to Germany and Japan at the expense of the U.S.S.R.; second—causing economic loss and damage to the U.S.S.R.; third—causing political damage to the U.S.S.R."   (Vol. VI, p. 49.)

On the instructions of the "bloc of Rights and Trotskyites" the accused SHARANGOVICH carried on extensive wrecking activities in agriculture and industry in the Byelorussian Soviet Socialist Republic.

On this matter the accused SHARANGOVICH testified as follows:

"For the purpose of putting our wrecking designs into effect we created in the local districts a network of wrecking and diversionist groups. . . . All of us, from the leaders of the organization down to the rank-and-file members, were national-fascists and carried on activities against the Soviet government for severing Byelorussia from the U.S.S.R., sticking at nothing in our efforts. . . ."   (Vol. XIV, p. 40.)

The accused CHERNOV, who for a number of years has been connected with the German intelligence service as one of its secret agents in the U.S.S.R., also took active advantage of the high official position he occupied in the U.S.S.R. to organize, on the instructions of the German intelligence service, a number of diversionist and wrecking acts in the sphere of agriculture. •

The accused CHERNOV, a German spy, giving testimony on his criminal connections with the German spy SCHEFFER, the correspondent of the "Berliner Tageblatt," and on his wrecking activities in the sphere of agriculture, stated the following:

"When I went to work at the Committee of Agricultural Stocks SCHEFFER conveyed to me the instructions of the Germans

---

*   Khrushchev has pronounced Tukhachevsky innocent and Krestinsky is rehabilitated, so this story collapses.

**   See above, page 31.

**   Chernov has been rehabilitated.

to carry on wrecking activities in the sphere of operations of
the Committee of Agricultural Stocks, particularly in regard
to mobilization reserves.

"The wrecking instructions I received from the intelligence service coincided with those which I, as a member of
the Right organization, had received from RYKOV. All the
more ready was I, therefore, to carry them out."
(Vol. VIII, pp. 98 reverse, 25.)

In respect to this, CHERNOV testified as follows:

"In 1934 I met RYKOV at his country house and he gave
me instructions to carry on wrecking activities on a wide
scale in the sphere of agriculture. I carried out these instructions and pursued wrecking and undermining activities
fairly actively."   (Vol. VIII, p. 93.)

The investigation has revealed considerable undermining
wrecking activities in the sphere of agriculture also in Uzbekistan, where the nationalist organizations, which, through their
✱   leaders, the accused IKRAMOV and KHODJAYEV, were in
alliance with the centre of the anti-Soviet conspiracy, operated.

The accused FAIZULLA KHODJAYEV, one of the leaders of
this nationalist organization, testified as follows:

"We did not confine ourselves only to preparing cadres
for our armed struggle against the Soviet power; we were
already actively working with the object of undermining the
power of the U.S.S.R."   (Vol. XIII, p. 66.)

The extensive application of wrecking measures in Uzbekistan
was also fully corroborated by the accused IKRAMOV, who testified that the "bloc of Rights and Trotskyites" had set him the
following tasks:

"...a) to make extensive preparations in Uzbekistan for
armed insurrection, to be started simultaneously with the
beginning of intervention;

"b) vigorously to carry on wrecking and diversionist operations in all branches of the national economy with a view
to their consequences rousing among the toilers discontent
with the Soviet power and thus creating favourable ground
for the organization of armed insurrection at the proper moment."

"In addition to this," the accused IKRAMOV stated, "the
object of our wrecking activities was to hinder the strengthen-
ing of the defence of the U.S.S.R." (Vol. XII, pp. 95-96.)

Wrecking activities in agriculture as well as in a number of
other branches of the national economy and Socialist construction
were also carried on by other accused in the present case.

✱   Ikramov and Khodjayev have been rehabilitated.

Thus, the accused GRINKO pursued wrecking activities in the sphere of finance.

The accused GRINKO testified as follows:

"The main object of undermining work in the People's Commissariat of Finance was the following: to weaken the Soviet ruble, to weaken the financial power of the U.S.S.R., to dislocate the economy and thus rouse among the population discontent with the financial policy of the Soviet power, discontent over taxes, discontent with the bad savings banks service, delays in paying wages, etc., which were to result in wide, organized discontent with the Soviet power and were to help the conspirators to recruit adherents and to develop insurrectionary activities." (Vol. IX, p. 79.)

The accused ZELENSKY and the group of wreckers he organized in the Centrosoyuz and the co-operative societies caused confusion in the planning of such goods as sugar, butter, eggs, makhorka, etc., deliberately held up the shipment of goods to the rural districts, utterly confused accounts, which facilitated the robbery and squandering of state funds with impunity, and encouraged the cheating and robbery of consumers.

Speaking of the wrecking system of accounting of goods and money he introduced in the Centrosoyuz, the accused ZELENSKY testified as follows:

"Under these circumstances the thief remained unpunished, while, owing to the complicated system of accounting, the honest worker got muddled up and was immediately accused of embezzlement." (Vol. X, p. 56.)

Treasonable wrecking activities on a considerable scale were also carried on by the now exposed agent of foreign intelligence services, the accused ROSENGOLTZ.

Concerning his treasonable activities in this sphere, the accused ROSENGOLTZ testified as follows:

"In so far as TROTSKY had an agreement with Germany and Japan, of which I had been informed (both during the negotiations—at my meeting with Sedov in 1933; and of the agreement that had been reached—at my meeting with him in 1934), I received corresponding instructions from TROTSKY, and my wrecking activities in the sphere of foreign trade served the same purpose." (Vol. VI, p. 48.)

Simultaneously with the organization of active diversionist and wrecking activities, the conspirators, on the orders of the fascist intelligence services, set themselves the task of rousing an insurrectionary bandit movement in our country with the object

---

*   Grinko has been rehabilitated.

**   Zelensky also has been rehabilitated.

of organizing an armed rising of their insurrectionary anti-Soviet gangs in the rear of the Red Army on the outbreak of intervention against the U.S.S.R.

The accused RYKOV testified as follows:

> "We took the course of the violent overthrow of the leadership of the Party and the Soviet power, and we decided to secure this overthrow by organizing kulak risings."
>
> (Vol. I, p. 150 reverse.)

The investigation has established that the kulak insurrectionary armed risings that were being organized to take place in the rear of the Red Army were part and parcel of the plans and calculations of the fascist states which were preparing to attack the U.S.S.R.; and that the Right and Trotskyite conspirators were preparing to rise at the signal of the General Staffs of the fascist countries.

Pursuing the instructions of the fascist intelligence services, the participants in the conspiracy collected insurrectionary bandit cadres, preparing them for an active armed rising in the Far East, the North Caucasus and other places in the Soviet Union, particularly in Uzbekistan.

*   On this matter the accused KHODJAYEV testified as follows:

> "The main object of the practical work of our organizations was to prepare active anti-Soviet cadres and to train them in the spirit of struggle against the U.S.S.R. We accustomed the members of the organization to the idea that the fight against the Soviet power would assume acute forms and would lead to armed conflicts. That is why we devoted attention to the preparation of the fighting forces of our organization."   (Vol. XIII, p. 66.)

The organizers of insurrectionary bandit cadres relied only on the remnants of the old counter-revolutionary elements, expecting to reinforce their insurrectionary reserves with the remnants of the Basmachis and White Guards, who were to be smuggled into the Soviet Union from abroad, and with criminal bandits, inmates of prison camps, etc.

Speaking of the insurrectionary bandit activities of the bourgeois nationalist organization headed by him in Uzbekistan, the
**   accused IKRAMOV testified:

> "We preserved the necessary cadres, which in future were to be utilized for an armed struggle against the Soviet power. These cadres consisted chiefly of remnants of the

---

*   But this accused has been rehabilitated.

**   ... and this one.

kulaks, priests and former Basmachis. We instructed the
members of our organization holding leading district posts
to preserve these cadres. Furthermore, we assumed that in
case of armed action the remnants of the Basmachi bands
which at one time had had to retreat across the frontier would
return to Soviet territory.''   (Vol. XII, p. 56.)

The materials of the investigation and the personal testimony
of the accused BUKHARIN, ZUBAREV, ZELENSKY and
others establish the fact that they had engaged in the active
training of insurrectionary cadres, attempting to cover as many
districts of the Soviet Union as possible, and that, with the purpose
of enlarging the insurrectionary base to the maximum, the leaders
of the conspiracy had established contact with an illegal Socialist-
Revolutionary organization.

Thus, the accused BUKHARIN testified:

"The establishment of connections with the Socialist-
Revolutionaries dates back to the period when the organization of the Rights placed its stakes on kulak risings. In view
of the fact that the Rights had embarked on the organization
of such risings, the necessity arose of establishing connections
with the Socialist-Revolutionaries, who had their roots in
the kulak strata in the countryside.

"... I personally established connections through SEM-
YONOV with the underground Central Committee of the
Socialist-Revolutionaries within the Soviet Union, and through
CHLENOV with the foreign Central Committee of the So-
cialist-Revolutionaries in Paris.''   (Vol. V, pp. 90-91.)

Such is the chain of shameful villainies perpetrated by the
"bloc of Rights and Trotskyites,'' which for many years carried
on its treasonable activities in the interests of foreign states
hostile to the U.S.S.R.

II. MURDER OF SOVIET PUBLIC MEN—S. M. KIROV, V. R. MENZHINSKY, V. V. KUIBYSHEV AND A. M. GORKY— PLOT AGAINST V. I. LENIN IN 1918

Entertaining no hope of the overthrow of the Soviet system by
means of espionage, wrecking, diversion, and kulak risings, the
Right and Trotskyite conspirators, possessed with rage and hatred for
the U.S.S.R., proceeded to make preparations for and to commit
terrorist acts against leaders of the government and the C.P.S.U.

The investigation has established the fact that by direct agreement with the Japanese and German intelligence services, and
upon the instructions of enemy of the people L. TROTSKY, the
"bloc of Rights and Trotskyites'' engineered and committed a number of terrorist acts against some of the finest people of our country.

The accused RYKOV explained the motives for the adoption
of terrorist methods by the "bloc of Rights and Trotskyites'' as
follows:

"In view of the illegal and conspiratorial character of the counter-revolutionary organization of the Rights, the absence of any kind of mass basis for its counter-revolutionary activities, and the absence of all hope of arriving at power in any other way, the adoption of terrorist methods and a 'palace coup d'état,' in the opinion of the Centre, held out some prospects."   (Vol. I, p. 50.)

The accused BUKHARIN, who in the course of the investigation admitted that the "bloc of Rights and Trotskyites" had already adopted terrorist methods in 1932, testified as follows:

"In 1932, too, during a meeting and conversation I had with PYATAKOV, I learnt from him of his meeting with L. SEDOV and his receipt through SEDOV of direct instructions from TROTSKY to adopt terrorist methods against leaders of the Party and the Soviet government. I must also confess that it was then that we virtually consented to an agreement with terrorists, and my conversation with PYATAKOV was an agreement to co-ordinate with TROTSKY our actions directed towards the forcible overthrow of the leadership of the Party and the Soviet government."
                                    (Vol. V, p. 105 reverse.)

The terrorist activities of the conspirators were closely connected with the whole of their defeatist work, which is borne out, for example, by the following testimony of the accused IVANOV:

"Speaking of terrorism, BUKHARIN said that the 'liquidation,' as he expressed it, of the leaders of the Party and the Soviet government . . . would be very important for our accession to power and would facilitate the defeat of the U.S.S.R. in war."   (Vol. VII, p. 81.)

In pursuance of the decisions taken in this connection, the conspiratorial bloc widely developed the organization of terrorist groups and the practical preparations for the perpetration of terrorist acts against leaders of the C.P.S.U. and the Soviet government.

This is what the accused RYKOV testified in this connection:

"By that time we had already adopted the path of terrorism as one of the methods of combating the Soviet government. . . . This position of ours took the form of quite definite activity on our part, and in particular on my part, in preparing terrorist acts against members of the Political Bureau, leaders of the Party and the government, and, first and foremost, against STALIN, MOLOTOV, KAGANOVICH and VOROSHILOV. In 1934 I had already given instructions to have the automobiles of leaders of the Party and the government watched by the ARTEMENKO terrorist group I had

---

*   Ivanov has been rehabilitated.

formed.''   (Vol. I, pp. 150 reverse, 151.)

Speaking of the proposal of the Socialist-Revolutionary SEMYO-NOV to organize a terrorist group, the accused BUKHARIN testified:

''I want to tell the truth and declare that this proposal was reported by me to a meeting of the centre, and we decided to charge SEMYONOV with the organization of terrorist groups.''   (Vol. V, p. 106 reverse.)

The investigation has established that the vile assassination of S. M. KIROV committed by the Leningrad Trotskyite-Zinovievite terrorist centre on December 1, 1934, was also committed in pursuance of a decision of the "bloc of Rights and Trotskyites," members of which are being charged in the present case.

The investigation has established that one of the participants in this vile murder was the accused YAGODA, who testified as follows:

''That preparations for the assassination of S. M. KIROV were being made in accordance with a decision of the conspiratorial centre, I had previously learnt from YENUKIDZE. YENUKIDZE told me not to hinder the organization of this terrorist act, and I agreed. With this purpose I summoned ZAPOROZHETZ from Leningrad and instructed him not to hinder the terrorist act that was being prepared against S. M. KIROV.''   (Vol. II, p. 209.)

This was confirmed by ZAPOROZHETZ and YENUKIDZE during the investigation.

The villainous terrorist activities of the Right and Trotskyite

---

*   Yenukidze has been rehabilitated, and eulogised in *Pravda:* "The Communist Party and the Soviet people profoundly revere his bright memory". (May 19th, 1962: see Nicolaevsky, *Power and the Soviet Elite,* pp.218 *et.seq.)* This nullifies Yagoda's testimony, and also Rykov's later evidence on the "murder" of Gorky. Gorky in fact had tuberculosis, and died at the age of 68. Isaac Babel was a constant visitor at Gorky's during the last few years of his life, and he told Ilya Ehrenburg that the whole story of Gorky's murder "was insane". Cf. Ehrenburg, in Novaya Zhizn, 1962, No.5, p.153, cited Ulam: *Stalin the Man and his Era,* Allen Lane 1973, p.484. On the other hand, Robert Conquest offers witness that Gorky was, indeed, poisoned, if not by the accused (p.539 *et.seq.).*

traitors and conspirators were not confined to the assassination of S. M. KIROV.

As the investigation of the present case has established, A. M. GORKY, V. R. MENZHINSKY and V. V. KUIBYSHEV fell victims to terrorist acts committed on the instructions of the Joint Centre of the "bloc of Rights and Trotskyites."

As to the reasons which induced the Right and Trotskyite conspirators to commit the unparalleled and monstrous murder of A. M. GORKY, the accused YAGODA testified:

> "For a long time the Joint Centre of the Right and Trotskyite organization had endeavoured to influence GORKY and make him sever his close connections with STALIN. For this purpose KAMENEV, TOMSKY and a number of others were attached to STALIN. But no real results were achieved. GORKY remained faithful to STALIN and was an ardent supporter and advocate of his line. As the overthrow of the STALIN leadership and the seizure of power by the Rights and Trotskyites was being considered seriously, the centre could not ignore the exceptional influence of GORKY within the country and his prestige abroad. If GORKY remained alive he would raise his voice in protest against us. That we could not allow. Having become convinced that GORKY could not be severed from STALIN, the Joint Centre, therefore, had to decide to do away with GORKY." (Vol. II, p. 200.)

The testimony of the accused YAGODA was fully corroborated by the accused RYKOV, who, when interrogated by the Procurator of the U.S.S.R. on January 10, 1938, testified:

> "I know that TROTSKY, through his representatives in the contact centre, did his utmost to fan animosity against GORKY. This is naturally to be explained by the fact that TROTSKY was well aware that GORKY considered him a scoundrel and adventurer. On the other hand, the close friendship of GORKY for STALIN was generally known, and the fact that he was an inflexible political supporter of STALIN aroused the animosity of our organization against him."
> (Vol. I, p. 166 reverse.)

To this the accused RYKOV added:

> "In 1935 I had a conversation with YENUKIDZE, who bluntly told me that the Trotskyite-Zinovievite part of the bloc insisted on eliminating the political activities of GORKY and would stop at nothing to attain this end. This conversation made it clear to me that the question of doing away with GORKY by terrorist methods might also arise."
> (Vol. I, pp. 166 reverse, 167.)

*

---

*   Yenukidze is, however, still rehabilitated.

This was also corroborated by the accused BUKHARIN, who
testified that in the beginning of 1935 TOMSKY had told him
that:

" . . . The Trotskyite part of the Joint Centre of the bloc
had proposed to organize a hostile act against A. M. GORKY
because he was a supporter of STALIN'S policy."

(Vol. V, p. 119 reverse.)

In this connection the accused BUKHARIN explained that
he does not preclude the possibility that it was the physical
removal of GORKY that was then contemplated. That preparations
for the physical removal of M. GORKY were contemplated
is shown by the testimony of the accused BESSONOV, who was
personally given a "line" to this effect directly by L. TROTSKY
when he met the latter at the end of July 1934.

The accused BESSONOV testified that at this meeting
L. TROTSKY, having declared that

" '. . . it would be unpardonable squeamishness if we did
not at once proceed to the systematic physical removal of
STALIN and of all his immediate colleagues,' said:

" 'M. GORKY is very intimate with STALIN. He plays
an exceptional role in winning sympathy for the U.S.S.R.
among the democratic opinion of the world and especially
of Western Europe. GORKY is very popular as a close friend
of STALIN'S and as a vehicle of the general line of the Party.
Our former supporters among the intelligentsia are leaving us very largely under the influence of GORKY. From this
I draw the conclusion that GORKY must be put out of the
way. Convey this instruction to PYATAKOV in the most
categorical form: GORKY must be physically exterminated
at all costs.' "   (Vol. XI, pp. 74-75.)

It was in accordance with this instruction of enemy of the people L. TROTSKY that the "bloc of Rights and Trotskyites"
adopted its monstrous decision to murder A. M. GORKY.

"The execution of this decision was entrusted to me,"
the accused YAGODA testified.

The accused YAGODA enlisted the accused in this case
Dr. L. G. LEVIN, former family doctor of A. M. GORKY, Professor
D. D. PLETNEV, P. P. KRYUCHKOV, A. M. GORKY'S secretary, and P. P. BULANOV, YAGODA'S own secretary, as the
immediate perpetrators of this villainous plan.

The accused BULANOV, one of the organizers of this crime,
testified:

"Professor PLETNEV, Dr. LEVIN and GORKY'S secretary, KRYUCHKOV, took a direct part in the killing of
A. M. GORKY. I, for instance, personally witnessed how YA-
GODA frequently summoned KRYUCHKOV and advised
him to cause GORKY to catch a chill, to make him fall ill
in one way or another. YAGODA stressed the point that the
condition of GORKY'S lungs was such that any illness caused

by a cold would increase the chances of his death. The rest would be done by PLETNEV and LEVIN, who had suitable instructions on this score."   (Vol. XVI, p. 72.)

The accused PLETNEV, who took a direct part in the murder of A. M. GORKY and V. V. KUIBYSHEV, testified:

"YAGODA told me that I must help him to secure the physical removal of certain political leaders of the country. He bluntly proposed that I should take advantage of my position as physician to V. V. KUIBYSHEV and A. M. GORKY to hasten their death by wrong methods of treatment. I attempted to refuse, but in the end was forced to consent. After this, YAGODA informed me that my accomplice would be Dr. LEVIN, and, in the case of A. M. GORKY, the latter's secretary, P. P. KRYUCHKOV, as well.

"Having accepted this gruesome commission from YAGODA, I, in conjunction with Dr. LEVIN, drew up a plan for the killing of A. M. GORKY and V. V. KUIBYSHEV.

"I must confess that my anti-Soviet sentiments played a part in my consent to this crime. Until my arrest I concealed these anti-Soviet sentiments in every way, playing a game of duplicity and claiming to be a Soviet supporter."
(Vol. XVIII, pp. 72-73.)

This was corroborated by the accused LEVIN, who testified:

"I confess that by deliberately adopting a wrong method of treatment and prescribing medicines unsuited to the given illness, I, together with my accomplices, and in agreement with YAGODA, was responsible for the untimely death of MAXIM GORKY and KUIBYSHEV." (Vol. XVII, p. 10.)

During the course of the investigation, the accused LEVIN and PLETNEV gave detailed testimony as to the way they actually arranged the killing of A. M. GORKY and V. V. KUIBYSHEV.

The investigation has established that the accused MAXIMOV, V. V. KUIBYSHEV'S secretary, took an active part in bringing about the death of V. V. KUIBYSHEV. MAXIMOV testified as follows:

"I consented to this crime as a member of the counter-revolutionary organization of the Rights, which I had joined in 1928.

"YAGODA also knew that I belonged to the counter-revolutionary organization and was present during one of my conversations with YENUKIDZE, when we drew up the plan for doing away with KUIBYSHEV."
(Vol. XX, p. 45 reverse.)

---

* Kryuchkov has been rehabilitated (See Medvedev, *ibid.)*

** But Yenukidze is now admitted to be innocent of this.

V. R. MENZHINSKY, Chairman of the O.G.P.U., was also murdered by the accused Dr. LEVIN and Dr. KAZAKOV on the direct instructions of YAGODA.

Interrogated by the Procurator of the U.S.S.R. on February 4, 1938, the accused KAZAKOV testified:

"YAGODA told me that MENZHINSKY liked and trusted me and that therefore Dr. LEVIN and I could succeed in doing away with MENZHINSKY. YAGODA gave me the following instructions: I was to work out with Dr. LEVIN a method of treatment for V. R. MENZHINSKY that would hasten his death and end his life as soon as possible. . . ."

(Vol. XIX, p. 51 reverse.)

Continuing to relate his conversation with the accused YAGODA in which the latter spoke of the necessity of hastening the death of V. R. MENZHINSKY, the accused KAZAKOV testified:

"After this conversation with YAGODA, LEVIN and I drew up a method of treatment for V. R. MENZHINSKY which in reality totally undermined his strength and determined the rapid onset of death. Thus LEVIN and I actually murdered V. R. MENZHINSKY in this way.

"I gave Dr. LEVIN a mixture of lysates I had composed, which, in conjunction with alkaloids, led to the desired result, namely, the virtual murder of MENZHINSKY."

(Vol. XIX, p. 51 reverse.)

This was fully corroborated by the accused L. G. LEVIN and P. P. BULANOV.

The accused L. G. LEVIN confirmed that, having received instructions from the accused YAGODA to hasten the death of V. R. MENZHINSKY, he, LEVIN, decided to enlist Dr. KAZAKOV in this crime.

The accused LEVIN testified:

"I said that this could be done best of all by KAZAKOV, as he used medicines which he himself prepared without control in his own laboratory, and what he injected he alone knew.

"After preliminary and preparatory talks with KAZAKOV, I conveyed to him the instructions I had received from YAGODA. He hesitated very much at first, fearing that the crime might be discovered, but in the end he consented. I did not ask what he used, all the more since he usually kept his medicines secret, but I knew that he had wide opportunities in this respect.

"V. R. MENZHINSKY'S death occurred suddenly during sleep from paralysis of the heart, on the eve of the death of MAXIM PESHKOV (A. M. GORKY'S son), if I am not mistaken. I had no doubt that this was KAZAKOV'S work."

(Vol. XVII, pp. 54-55.)

On the subject of the murder of V. R. MENZHINSKY, the accused BULANOV testified:

"YAGODA had long ago conceived the idea of physically removing MENZHINSKY. He several times in my presence expressed dissatisfaction that MENZHINSKY continued to live and to occupy the post of head of the O.G.P.U. Then he said outright that MENZHINSKY must be put out of the way. It was difficult to arrange the job through Dr. LEVIN, because MENZHINSKY did not like LEVIN and refused to be treated by him. I then suggested to YAGODA to 'fix up' some other doctor for MENZHINSKY. This was done. With the assistance of Dr. LEVIN, MENZHINSKY was 'fixed up' with Dr. KAZAKOV, who did the job, or, to put it plainly, hastened MENZHINSKY'S death by deliberately employing a wrong method of treatment."   (Vol. XVI, p. 75.)

Apart from the murder of A. M. GORKY and V. V. KUIBY-SHEV, the accused LEVIN and KRYUCHKOV, on direct instructions of the accused YAGODA, in 1934 killed M. A. PESHKOV, the son of A. M. GORKY, in a similar way.

In this connection, the accused LEVIN testified:

"I confess my guilt in the murder of Maxim and want to say here that I did it on the direct demand of YAGODA. I did not have the courage to refuse, and I became a murderer."
(Vol. XVII, p. 138 reverse.)

The accused KRYUCHKOV, who took an active part in the crimes organized by YAGODA, testified:

"In these crimes I was guided by the directions of certain members of the anti-Soviet organization of the Rights, in particular by the directions of YAGODA. It was from YA-GODA that I received instructions forcibly to do away with Maxim PESHKOV, and then Alexei Maximovich GORKY.

"In addition to myself, YAGODA enlisted for the commission of these crimes the physicians LEVIN and VINOGRA-DOV and Professor PLETNEV."   (Vol. XXI, p. 16.)

The accused YAGODA, confirming that M. A. PESHKOV was murdered on his instructions, testified:

"In May 1934, with the help of KRYUCHKOV, Max (M. A. PESHKOV) contracted double pneumonia, and the physicians LEVIN, VINOGRADOV and PLETNEV treated him in such a way as to bring about his death."   (Vol. II, p. 193.)

After being removed from his post as People's Commissar of Internal Affairs of the U.S.S.R., the accused YAGODA also took

---

*   Kryuchkov has been rehabilitated.

measures to murder Comrade N. I. YEZHOV, People's Commissar
* of Internal Affairs of the U.S.S.R.

In his testimony, the accused YAGODA explained the motives
which induced him to hasten a terrorist act against N. I. YEZHOV
as follows:

> "My removal from my post in the People's Commissariat
> of Internal Affairs and the appointment of YEZHOV in my
> place meant the complete collapse of our conspiracy, because
> it would be impossible to prevent the routing of the cadres
> of the anti-Soviet organization. YEZHOV would dig up every-
> thing. YEZHOV had to be put out of the way. This was the
> only decision I could come to, and I began to make energetic
> preparations to put it into effect...." (Vol. II, pp. 141-42.)

YAGODA attempted to carry out his plan through his accomplices, a prominent part being played by the accused BULANOV.

The accused YAGODA and the accused BULANOV confessed
that it was proposed to accomplish the murder of Comrade N. I.
YEZHOV by means of a poison specially prepared for the purpose:

> "When YAGODA was removed from the People's Commis-
> sariat of Internal Affairs," the accused BULANOV testified,
> "he gave me and his personal agent, SAVOLAINEN, direct
> instructions to poison YEZHOV."   (Vol. XVI, p. 27.)

Describing in detail the methods by which the accused YA-
GODA tried to murder Comrade N. I. YEZHOV, the accused BU-
LANOV testified that he (BULANOV) himself prepared the mix-
ture of drugs intended for the poisoning of Comrade YEZHOV.

Interrogated in the Office of the Procurator of the U.S.S.R.,
the accused YAGODA fully admitted having committed this
crime, testifying:

> "Yes, I must admit that I made preparations for the per-
> petration of this crime. I made preparations for the murder
> of YEZHOV as a man who was dangerous to the counter-revo-
> lutionary plot and who might expose our counter-revolutionary
> organization."   (Vol. II, p. 209.)

Thus the investigating authorities consider it established beyond

---

* Yezhov's dispatch was subsequently successfully accomplished, by Stalin. Later he told Yakolev "Yezhov was a
scoundrel. He killed our best people. The man went to the
dogs. You call him at the Ministry, they say he has gone to
the Central Committee. Call him there, they say he is at
work. You send after him to his house, he is lying in bed
dead drunk. How many people he destroyed! For that we
had him shot". Yakovlev, cited Ulam, *Stalin,* p.487.

all doubt that the leading members of the "bloc of Rights and Trotskyites," against whom criminal proceedings are being brought in this case, committed terrorist acts against S. M. KIROV, V. R. MENZHINSKY, V. V. KUIBYSHEV, A. M. GORKY and M. A. PESHKOV and made preparations for a number of other terrorist acts which they had no time to carry out.

The murder of Soviet public men completed the circle of heinous state crimes by which this band of contemptible apostates of our country, provocateurs of the tsarist secret police and hirelings of foreign intelligence services, who were selling our land and liberty to foreign capitalists, strove to carry out a fascist plan for the overthrow of the Soviet system and the restoration of capitalism in our country.

As has now been brought to light, neither in the case of the Trotskyites nor in the case of the Rights were these monstrous crimes fortuitous.

The investigation has established that as far back as 1918, directly after the October Revolution, at the time of the conclusion of the Peace of Brest-Litovsk, BUKHARIN and his group of so-called "Left Communists," and TROTSKY and his group, together with the "Left" Socialist-Revolutionaries, hatched a plot against V. I. LENIN, the head of the Soviet government.

As the materials of the investigation show, BUKHARIN and other conspirators aimed at frustrating the Brest-Litovsk Peace, overthrowing the Soviet government, arresting and murdering V. I. LENIN, J. V. STALIN and J. M. SVERDLOV, and forming a new government consisting of Bukharinites—who as a blind at that time called themselves "Left Communists"—of Trotskyites and of "Left" Socialist-Revolutionaries.

Questioned in the Office of the Procurator of the U.S.S.R. on February 19 and 20, 1938, V. A. KARELIN, former member of the Central Committee of the Party of "Left" Socialist-Revolutionaries, gave the following testimony regarding the conspiratorial activities of the Socialist-Revolutionaries and Bukharinites in 1918:

> "Final agreement with the 'Left Communists' in the struggle against the Soviet government headed by LENIN, STALIN and SVERDLOV was reached by us after the Seventh Congress of the Communist Party.
>
> "On the instructions of the Central Committee of the 'Left' Socialist-Revolutionaries, the negotiations with the 'Left Communists' were conducted by KAMKOV, PROSHYAN, and myself."   (Vol. XLIV, p. 86.)

Speaking of the character of these negotiations and the part played by the accused N. I. BUKHARIN, V. A. KARELIN further testified as follows:

> "BUKHARIN proposed that we should not stop at the

arrest of the government but bring about the physical extermination of the leaders of the Soviet power, and in the first
place of LENIN and STALIN.''   (Vol. XLIV, p. 38.)

This was corroborated by other persons who were examined as
witnesses in the present case.

B. D. KAMKOV, one of the former leaders of the Central Committee of the "Left" Socialist-Revolutionary Party, testified:

"I personally had a conversation with BUKHARIN in
which he said roughly the following: 'The struggle within our
Party against LENIN'S position on the Brest-Litovsk Peace
is assuming acute forms. Within our ranks the question is being
discussed of creating a new government consisting of "Left"
Socialist-Revolutionaries and "Left Communists."'' BUKHA-
RIN mentioned PYATAKOV as a possible candidate for leader
of the new government, and stated that the idea was to bring
about the change of government by arresting its members,
headed by LENIN.

"Further negotiations with BUKHARIN were conducted
by KARELIN and PROSHYAN. By the end of March a final
agreement was reached between the 'Left Communists' and
the 'Left' Socialist-Revolutionaries on the following points:
1) that in the struggle against the Bolsheviks and the Soviet
government the 'Left Communists' were to render organization-
al and political assistance to the 'Left' Socialist-Revolutionaries; 2) that by joint action of the 'Left' Socialist-Revolutionaries and 'Left Communists,' LENIN'S government was to
be overthrown and a new government formed, consisting of
'Left Communists' and 'Left' Socialist-Revolutionaries.

"After this, the 'Left' Socialist-Revolutionaries organized
the assassination of MIRBACH and the July revolt. The 'Left
Communists' were fully aware of the preparations being made
for the assassination of MIRBACH and for the July revolt."
(Vol. XLIV, p. 92 reverse.)

Questioned in the capacity of witnesses in the Office of the
Procurator of the U.S.S.R. on February 19, 1938, V. N. YAKOV-
LEVA, V. V. OSSINSKY and V. N. MANTSEV, former leaders and
active members of the group of "Left Communists," fully corroborated that in 1918 a plot was hatched, on the initiative of the
accused BUKHARIN, by the bloc of "Left Communists" and
"Left" Socialist-Revolutionaries against V. I. LENIN as head of
the Soviet government:

Thus, V. N. YAKOVLEVA testified:

"BUKHARIN expressed to me the idea that the political struggle was assuming ever more acute forms and that
matters could not be confined to the mere political formulation
of lack of confidence in the Central Committee of the Party.
BUKHARIN declared that a change of leadership was inevitable, and that in this connection the question was being
discussed of arresting LENIN, STALIN and SVERDLOV, and

*

2) RYKOV, Alexei Ivanovich, born 1881;
3) YAGODA, Genrikh Grigorievich, born 1891;
4) KRESTINSKY, Nikolai Nikolayevich, born 1883;
5) RAKOVSKY, Khristian Georgievich, born 1873;
6) ROSENGOLTZ, Arkady Pavlovich, born 1889;

7) IVANOV, Vladimir Ivanovich, born 1893;
8) CHERNOV, Mikhail Alexandrovich, born 1891;
9) GRINKO, Grigori Fedorovich, born 1890;
10) ZELENSKY, Isaac Abramovich, born 1890;
11) BESSONOV, Sergei Alexeyevich, born 1892;
12) IKRAMOV, Akmal, born 1898;
13) KHODJAYEV, Faizulla, born 1896;
14) SHARANGOVICH, Vasily Fomich, born 1897;
15) ZUBAREV, Prokopy Timofeyevich, born 1886;
16) BULANOV, Pavel Petrovich, born 1895;
17) LEVIN, Lev Grigorievich, born 1870;
18) PLETNEV, Dmitry Dmitrievich, born 1872;
19) KAZAKOV, Ignaty Nikolayevich, born 1891;
20) MAXIMOV-DIKOVSKY, Venyamin Adamovich (Abramovich), born 1900;

**

21) KRYUCHKOV, Pyotr Petrovich, born 1889.
—are accused of having, as active participants in an anti-Soviet conspiracy, committed the gravest state crimes enumerated in paragraphs 1-5 of the Definition of the Charge, i.e., crimes covered by Articles 58^{1a}, 58^2, 58^7, 58^8, 58^9, and 58^{11} of the Criminal Code of the R.S.F.S.R., and the accused IVANOV, ZELENSKY and ZUBAREV, in addition, of crimes covered by Article 58^{13} of the Criminal Code of the R.S.F.S.R.

On the aforesaid grounds all the above-mentioned accused are subject to trial by the Military Collegium of the Supreme Court of the U.S.S.R.

The cases of V. V. OSSINSKY, V. N. YAKOVLEVA, V. N. MANTSEV, V. A. KARELIN, B. D. KAMKOV, I. N. STUKOV, E. V. ARTEMENKO, I. V. ZAPOROZHETZ, I. M. SAVOLAINEN, G. I. SEMYONOV and S. B. CHLENOV have been made the subject of separate proceedings.

Proceedings against Dr. A. I. VINOGRADOV have been terminated owing to his death.

The case of A. S. YENUKIDZE was tried by the Military Collegium of the Supreme Court of the U.S.S.R. on December 15, 1937.

The present indictment was drawn up in Moscow on February 23, 1938.

A. VYSHINSKY
Procurator of the U.S.S.R.

---

* As is Rykov.

** So close-woven is the plot of this scenario that the rehabilitation of seven of the twenty-one leaves it in tatters.

In addition, off-stage as it were, Yenukidze and Rudzutak, Tukhachevsky and his colleagues, the Poles, and various other posthumous acquittals, leave little unanswered but the preposterous conspiracy against Lenin, which does not figure in the final definition of the charge.

Of course, all this stew of accusations is as tedious as it is poisonous. It would have been quicker to call a single witness. Recording his memoirs on tape in enforced retirement, N.S. Khrushchev said:

"Just before the Twentieth Party Congress I summoned the State Prosecutor, Comrade Rudenko, who has been involved in many of the cases during the purges of the thirties. I asked him, "Comrade Rudenko, I'm interested in the open trials. Tell me, how much basis in actual fact was there for the accusations made against Bukharin, Rykov, Syrtsov, Lominadze, Krestinsky, and many, many other people well known to the Central Committee, to the Orgbureau, and to the Politbureau?"

Comrade Rudenko answered that from the standpoint of judicial norms, there was no evidence whatsoever for condemning or even trying those men. The case for prosecuting them had been based on personal confessions beaten out of them under physical and psychological torture, and confessions extracted by such means are unacceptable as a legitimate basis for bringing someone to trial.

Nevertheless, we decided not to say anything about the open trials in my speech to the Twentieth Party Congress. There was a certain ambiguity in our conduct here. The reason for our decision was that there had been representatives of the fraternal Communist parties present when Rykov, Bukharin, and other leaders of the people were tried and sentenced. These representatives had then gone home and testified in their own countries to the justice of the sentences. We didn't want to discredit the fraternal Party representatives who had attended the open trials, so we indefinitely postponed the rehabilitation of Bukharin, Zinoviev, Rykov and the rest. I can see now that our decision was a mistake. It would have been better to tell

by the Central Committee of the Right Socialist-Revolutionaries.''   (Vol. XLIV, pp. 86-87.)

This was also corroborated by V. V. OSSINSKY, who, when
interrogated on February 19, 1938, testified as follows:

"At the end of 1918 STUKOV, who together with BUKHA-
RIN was connected with the Socialist-Revolutionaries, told
me that the shot fired at LENIN by the Right Socialist-Revolutionary KAPLAN was the result not only of the instructions of the leadership of the Right Socialist-Revolutionaries,
but also of measures that had been outlined by the bloc of
'Left Communists' with the Socialist-Revolutionaries aiming
at the physical extermination of LENIN, STALIN and
SVERDLOV.''   (Vol. XLIV, p. 89.)

At confrontations in the Office of the Procurator of the U.S.S.R.
of the accused BUKHARIN with the witnesses V. V. OSSINSKY,
V. N. YAKOVLEVA, V. N. MANTSEV, V. A. KARELIN and
B. D. KAMKOV, these witnesses fully confirmed their testimony
as set forth above.

Under the weight of the evidence, the accused BUKHARIN
admitted a number of criminal facts and testified:

"I must admit that we had direct contact with the 'Left'
Socialist-Revolutionaries, whose platform was the forcible
overthrow of the Soviet government, headed by LENIN,
STALIN and SVERDLOV, to be followed by the arrest of
LENIN, STALIN and SVERDLOV and the setting up of a new
government consisting of 'Left Communists' and 'Left' Socialist-Revolutionaries. . . .''   (Vol. V, p. 122 reverse.)

The facts now established regarding the crimes committed by
the accused BUKHARIN and enemy of the people TROTSKY in
1918 against the Soviet state and its leaders, V. I. LENIN, J. V.
STALIN and J. M. SVERDLOV, throw a vivid light on the whole
subsequent criminal counter-revolutionary activity of the gang of
BUKHARIN and TROTSKY, which is now charged with the
gravest state crimes committed on the direct instructions of fascist
intelligence services during the period 1921-1937.

DEFINITION OF THE CHARGE

The investigating authorities consider it established:
1) that in 1932-33, on the instructions of intelligence services of
foreign states hostile to the U.S.S.R., a conspiratorial group named
the "bloc of Rights and Trotskyites" was formed by the accused in the
present case with the object of espionage on behalf of foreign states,
wrecking, diversionist and terrorist activities, undermining the
military power of the U.S.S.R., provoking a military attack by
these states on the U.S.S.R., working for the defeat of the U.S.S.R.,
dismembering the U.S.S.R. and severing from it the Ukraine, Byelorussia, the Central Asiatic Republics, Georgia, Armenia, Azerbaijan and the Maritime Region of the Far East for the benefit

of the aforementioned foreign states, and, lastly, with the object
of overthrowing the Socialist social and state system existing in
the U.S.S.R. and of restoring capitalism and the power of the

* bourgeoisie in the U.S.S.R.;

   2) that the "bloc of Rights and Trotskyites" entered into relations
with certain foreign states with the purpose of receiving armed assist-

** ance from them for the accomplishment of its criminal designs;

   3) that the "bloc of Rights and Trotskyites" systematically engaged in espionage on behalf of these states, supplying foreign intelli-

*** gence services with highly important state secret information;

   4) that the "bloc of Rights and Trotskyites" systematically per-
formed wrecking and diversionist acts in various branches of Socialist construction (industry, agriculture, railways, in the sphere of

*† finance, municipal development, etc.);

   5) that the "bloc of Rights and Trotskyites" organized a number of
terrorist acts against leaders of the C.P.S.U. and the Soviet government and perpetrated terrorist acts against S. M. KIROV,

*‡ V. R. MENZHINSKY, V. V. KUIBYSHEV and A. M. GORKY.

   All the accused stand convicted both by the testimony of witnesses and by the documents and material evidence in the files
and have fully admitted that they are guilty of the charges preferred
against them.

   On the aforementioned grounds the following persons:

‡† 1) BUKHARIN, Nikolai Ivanovich, born 1888;

---

* As will be seen above, these charges have all been falsified.

** The exoneration of Krestinsky and Tukhachevsky leaves
a great hole in these charges, which can no longer be
sustained.

*** At an all-Union Conference of Historians in 1964, Central
Committee Secretary, Pospelov, said, in reply to a question,
that "neither Bukharin nor Rykov were spies or wreckers".
(Conquest, p.690: Medvedev, op.cit.).

*† Bukharin's denials in the Trial proper are all corroborated
by the crumbling of this evidence under the weight of
posthumous rehabilitations.

*‡ These charges, too, are honeycombed with holes made by
rehabilitations.

‡† Bukharin is denied posthumous rehabilitation.

even of their physical extermination. . . .''
(Vol. XLIV, p. 77.)

In this connection V. V. OSSINSKY testified as follows:

"It was with N. I. BUKHARIN that I principally talked about our measures for the overthrow of LENIN'S government. . . . Approximately in May (or at the end of April) 1918 I had a talk with BUKHARIN when I asked him to what extent the information I had about his designs to arrest the LENIN government was correct.

"BUKHARIN did not deny that he had such designs.''
(Vol. XLIV, p. 54.)

Speaking further about these "measures,'' V. V. OSSINSKY testified:

"I learned about the bloc of the 'Left Communists' with the 'Left' Socialist-Revolutionaries from YAKOVLEVA and then from BUKHARIN. I also learned from them that in March or April 1918 BUKHARIN proposed at the bureau (of the Moscow region) that LENIN, STALIN and SVERDLOV should be arrested. BUKHARIN further stressed the point that he was of the opinion that after the arrest of the government, LENIN, STALIN and SVERDLOV should be physically exterminated.''   (Vol. XLIV, p. 88 reverse.)

Similar testimony was given by V. N. MANTSEV when questioned in the Office of the Procurator of the U.S.S.R. on February 20, 1938:

"I confirm that a bloc was formed between the 'Left Communists' and 'Left' Socialist-Revolutionaries.

"I confirm that roughly in March or April, at a close meeting of the bureau, BUKHARIN made a report in which he uttered a number of slanderous statements against the Soviet government and proposed to organize the overthrow of the Soviet power and the arrest of LENIN, STALIN and SVERDLOV, with the purpose of physically exterminating them.''   (Vol. XLIV, p. 82.)

Speaking of the role of L. TROTSKY in the plot against V. I. LENIN in 1918, the accused BUKHARIN testified:

"At that time the idea again arose of a coup and the arrest of LENIN, STALIN and SVERDLOV as the dominant figures in the Party and Soviet leadership. This time it arose on the initiative of TROTSKY, to whom the proposal of the 'Left' Socialist-Revolutionaries apparently became known— through PYATAKOV, I presume.''   (Vol. V, p. 124.)

Interrogated during the preliminary investigation, V. N. YAKOVLEVA testified:

"TROTSKY considered that the political struggle had only just begun, that it might assume the most aggressive

forms, that against LENIN'S position on the question
of peace the 'Left Communists' would have the support of the 'Left' Socialist-Revolutionaries and other parties,
that preparations must be made for a change of government
and the arrest of its leaders, headed by LENIN and STALIN.
TROTSKY considered that in so acute a period of the revolution, if the struggle were to develop, matters might not be confined only to the arrest of the leaders, and that the arrests
would logically and inevitably lead to the question of their
physical removal." (Vol. XLIV, p. 78.)

Interrogated in the preliminary investigation, V. N. MANTSEV,
one of the leaders of the group of "Left Communists," testified:

"Several days after my conversation with YAKOVLEVA,
TROTSKY asked me to come and see him. I had a long talk
with him at his home, during which TROTSKY developed at
length the idea that LENIN and STALIN must be assassinated." (Vol. XLIV, p. 84.)

The investigating authorities now possess irrefutable evidence
proving that the villainous attempt on the life of V. I. LENIN committed on August 30, 1918, by the Socialist-Revolutionary terrorist F. KAPLAN was a direct result of the realization of the criminal plans of the "Left Communists," headed by N. I. BUKHA-
RIN, and of their accomplices, the "Left" and Right Socialist-
Revolutionaries, and was initiated by the accused BUKHARIN.

Questioned in the Office of the Procurator of the U.S.S.R. on
February 19, 1938, V. A. KARELIN testified:

"I must also confess to the gravest crime, namely, the
participation of the 'Left' Socialist-Revolutionaries and the
'Left Communists' in the organization of the attempt on the
life of LENIN. This fact has been concealed from the Soviet
people for twenty years. The fact was concealed that we, in
conjunction with the Right Socialist-Revolutionaries, on the
insistence of BUKHARIN, attempted to murder LENIN. The
trial of the Right Socialist-Revolutionaries did not disclose
the real circumstances of this crime and did not reveal the
part played in it by the 'Left' Socialist-Revolutionaries and
the 'Left Communists.'

"After the July revolt, the Central Committee of the 'Left'
Socialist-Revolutionaries decided to adopt terrorist methods in
the struggle against the Soviet government.

"It should be mentioned that even after the revolt PROSH-
YAN had meetings with BUKHARIN, who bluntly put before
him the question of the physical extermination of LENIN. More
precisely, the question of committing a terrorist act against
LENIN was raised by BUKHARIN in the second half of July
1918. PROSHYAN reported this to us members of the Central
Committee of the 'Left' Socialist-Revolutionaries.

"Such a demand by the 'Left Communists' played a great
part in hastening the terrorist act against LENIN committed

everything. Murder will always out. You can't keep things like that a secret for long".[1]

FOOTNOTES

1. *Khrushchev Remembers,* Andre Deutsch, 1971, pp.352-3. This book was repudiated by Khrushchev when the first volume appeared in the USA: but the second (subsequent) volume contained explanatory evidence about the circumstances of its publication which validate it as his work, at any rate in large measure. The book was prepared from tapes which Khrushchev dictated from memory, so that there is room for double error: it could be mistakenly edited in transcription, and it could be wrong because of Krushchev's faulty recollection and the absence of necessary documentation. There is, however, no room in this particular passage for errors of either sort, and we can take it that this actually was what Khrushchev said.

The five marshalls of the Soviet Union left to right — Tukhachevsky, Budenny, Voroshilov, Blucher, Yegorov.

Key architects of the Moscow Trials included, besides
Stalin, Vyshinsky *top left* (the prosecutor) and successive
NKVD chiefs, Yagoda *top right,* and Yezhov *bottom left.*
Yezhov was succeeded by Beria *bottom right.*

"There was no so-called 'internal aggression' in Russia co-operating with the German High Command. Hitler's march into Prague into 1939 was accompanied by the active military support of Henlein's organisations in Czechoslovakia. The same thing was true of his invasion of Norway. There were no Sudeten Henleins, no Slovakian Tisos, no Belgian De Grelles, no Norwegian Quislings in the Russian picture . . .

The story had been told in the so-called treason or purge trials of 1937 and 1938 which I attended and listened to. In re-examining the record of these cases and also what I had written at the time . . . I found that practically every device of German Fifth Columnist activity, as we now know it, was disclosed and laid bare by the confessions and testimony elicited at these trials of self-confessed 'Quislings' in Russia . . .

All of these trials, purges, and liquidations, which seemed so violent at the time and shocked the world, are now quite clearly a part of a vigorous and determined effort of the Stalin government to protect itself from not only revolution from within but from attack from without. They went to work thoroughly to clean up and clean out all treasonable elements within the country. All doubts were resolved in favour of the government.

There were no Fifth Columnists in Russia in 1941 – they had shot them. The purge had cleansed the country and rid it of treason.

The Axis Fifth Column in Soviet Russia had been smashed."[12]

Davies was totally wrong, of course: in spite of the infamy of Hitler's occupation of Soviet territories huge numbers of Soviet citizens were recruited into the army of the renegade General Vlasov. On the other hand, the pre-war extinction of the Red Army's most brilliant leaders undoubtedly weakened the Soviet resistance to invasion. Be that as it may, the world's most powerful capitalist nation was represented in the USSR by a man who was quite ready to believe Stalin's most blatant falsifications, so it is clear that Communist Parties were not alone in their misdeeds.

Unfortunately, there were far more plausible socialist advocates to lend support to the conspiracy theory. Notably, the Webbs swallowed the package whole, and were widely quoted in support of the necessity of repression.

Writing in their postscript to the second edition of *Soviet Communism, a New Civilisation,* Sidney and Beatrice Webb were able to speak in the same detached voices which had earlier laid bare the mysteries of the English Poor Law and the virtues of British trade unions. Calm, equable, totally devoid of the frenzy to be found in many Communist Party pronouncements, they lent their considerable authority to buttress the case of Vishinsky against the old Bolshevik leaders. After the earlier trials they had deliberately removed the question mark from the title of their last major book. Now they summed up:

"In December 1934 the head Bolshevik official in Leningrad (Kirov) was assassinated by a dismissed employee, who may have acted independently out of personal revenge, but who was discovered to have secret connections with conspiratorial circles of ever-widening range. The Government reaction to this murder was to hurry on the trial, condemnation and summary execution of the hundred or more persons above referred to, who were undoubtedly guilty of illegal entry and inexcusably bearing arms and bombs, although it was apparently not proved that they had any connection with Kirov's assassination or the conspiracies associated therewith. These conspiracies were gradually unravelled in several successive trials during 1936, which involved the condemnation and summary execution of Kamenev, Zinoviev and others of lesser notoriety.

A climax which seemed final was reached by the criminal proceedings in January 1937 against such leading Bolsheviks as Pyatakov, Serebryatakov, Radek and Sokolnikov, with others less well known abroad, upon charges of conspiracy to overthrow the Goverment by force, treasonable associations with German and Japanese government agents to this end, attempts at assassination of Molotov and other leaders, and criminal sabotage of mine and railway working resulting in loss of life. Yet only a few months later came a new sensation, when eight generals of the Red Army were tried and condemned to death for treasonable association with the emissaries and spies of foreign governments preparing for invasion of the USSR. The unpleasant impression of these proceedings on the western world was deepened by the bias persistently shown against the exiled Leon Trotsky, constantly alleged to have been the chief instigator and director of the whole series of crimes. The confessions of the defendants; the manner in which their several stories corroborated one another; their frank explanations of the way they had yielded to the temptation of giving their general adhesion to a treasonable conspiracy of which they did not at first understand the scope; and how they had then found themselves unable to escape from the toils in which they had become entangled; – be it added, a certain amount of further corroboration deduced from incautiously published utterances both by German and by Japanese statesmen, convinced the British and American journalists present at the trial in January 1937 that the defendants were really guilty of the treasonable conspiracies with which they were charged. Careful perusal of the full reports of the proceedings and speeches at the

Such was Pollitt's faith in the Soviet Government at that
time that one might easily believe that no conceivable
villainy on its part would call forth a protest from him.
Indeed, in the same article, he speaks enthusiastically of
"the Stalins, Molotovs, Kaganovitchs, Yezhovs, these are
the men of steel . . ."[4]

By contrast, Khrushchev tells us:

"Beria didn't create Stalin, Stalin created Beria. And before him,
Stalin created Yezhov. 'The Blackberry' and 'the Mailed Fist' —
these were Stalin's nicknames for Yezhov. And before Yezhov, there
was Yagoda. Stalin created Yagoda, too. One by one they made
their entrances and exits. The rapid turnover among the main
characters created by Stalin was very much part of Stalin's logic. He
used henchmen to destroy honest men who he knew perfectly well
were guiltless in the eyes of the Party and the people. Then Stalin
stood above it all while the terror consumed its own executors.
When one band of thugs got too embroiled in the terror, he simply
replaced it with another. That's how the three echelons came about:
first Yagoda, then Yezhov, then Beria . . ."[5]

To do him justice, Pollitt never contested the downfall
of any of these monsters, after it had been accomplished.
But until it became an accomplished fact, each in turn was
'a man of steel'.

Englishmen should not believe that Pollitt was exceptionally gullible or corrupt. Hardly any major Comintern
leader escaped the relentless pressure to endorse these trials
in similar terms. Dimitrov, considering the Zinoviev trial,
had set the framework for the official communist reaction:

"The trial of the terrorists, who are agents of Fascism, is an in-
tegral part of the struggle of the international working class against
fascism."[6]

That Dimitrov himself was the hero of the Reichstag
Trial in Hitler's Germany was, for any in Western Europe
who were not agnostic, a material guarantee of the sound-
ness of this judgement. Writing in the journal *Communist
International,* Togliatti spoke of "bandits" plotting "sacri-
ligious crimes", and identified the 1936 opening trial as "a
touchstone of our class vigilance".[7] Years later, in an interview given on 16 June 1956, Togliatti still hankered after

some foundation in fact for all the Trials, if rather more
tentatively than had been his earlier wont:

"It is still not clear to us whether the current denunciations of the
violation of legality and application of illegitimate and morally
repugnant prosecuting methods extend to the entire period of the
trials, or only to a given period, more recent than that to which I
have referred . . .

I repeat, with respect to the initial trials — which we were able
to consider, the later trials for the most part not being public — my
opinion today is that there existed simultaneously two elements:
the conspiratorial attempts of the opponents against the regime to
commit terrorist acts; and the application of illegal prosecuting
methods, censurable on a moral basis. The first, naturally, does not
minimise the gravity of the second."[8]

To give him his due, Togliatti apparently assumed
that some effort would be made, following Khrushchev's
revelations, to determine the extent to which such a mixture
had really existed, and to reassess the verdicts of at any rate
the "later" trials. No such concern for justice can be found
in the much more recent memoirs of D.N. Pritt, who was
one of the most prominent fellow travellers to justify the
first trial, in a veritable rash of articles and pamphlets, and
to dignify a Left Book Club account of the second trial
with an approving foreword.[9] At the end of a boastful
account of his attendance at the 1936 Trial, he appends a
short note about contemporary Soviet attitudes:

"What their views of the case now are, after the revelations made at
the Twentieth Congress . . . of the tragic abuses of the Stalin period,
I do not know. I have thought it best to leave unchanged my account
of the trial . . ."[10]

Curiosity was not a consuming passion for Mr Pritt, nor
for a whole number of more distinguished commentors on
the same themes.

No one should think that uncritical acceptance of the
official view in the USSR was confined to Communists:
not only Churchill[11] but Ambassador Davies of the United
States tended to accept that "wreckers" had indeed been at
work. Here, for instance, is just one of the Ambassador's
apercues:

CHAPTER IV

Guilty, Worldwide

Khrushchev's sensitivity to the feelings of the leaders of foreign Communist parties was not only prudent: it was founded in a circumstance which must be understood in order to comprehend the full significance of international opinion in this argument. By the time that the Soviet leaders had decided to denounce some of the most evil parts of the Stalin inheritance, it was proper to speak of "fraternal party representatives" because each Communist party had become constitutionally independent of the others, even if all shared a strong community of ideological commitment. But at the time of the Moscow Trials the Communist movement was still compassed within the framework of a single world-wide organisation, the Comintern, which possessed authority over all constituent national parties. Consequently there was no such thing as a purely "Russian" policy on the Trials: Comintern direction still existed, and the whole work of defending and apologising for the purges was an imperative mandate binding on all member organisations. That the Comintern had been completely incorporated under Soviet tutelage is beyond doubt: before he could be victimised by his Soviet colleagues Bukharin might well, in earlier days, have sought to launch an appeal to the Comintern, as this was, ostensibly, in communist lore, a juridically higher body than the Central Committee of the CPSU. Such a thought never dawned on anyone in the actual event, since it was plain that the whole Comintern machine was in fact subordinate not only to the Soviet authorities, but thus to Stalin personally. For this reason, foreign Communists (and non-Communists) played a major role in whitewashing the Trials. Writing within hours of Bukharin's execution, Harry Pollitt said:

"The trial of the 21 political and moral degenerates in Moscow is a mighty demonstration to the world of the power and strength of the Soviet Union . . .

All the groups within the Soviet Union who doubted the capacity of the Government to construct Socialism, groups who lost faith and could go no further in the hard fight to overcome difficulties, groups defeated in political struggles as to which policy should be followed by the Soviet Government all tended to draw together, and by their infamous activities conspired to hinder or destroy the great structure that millions were devoting their lives to build.

When fascism rose to power in Germany, and the militarist fascist regime in Japan gained strength – these two countries were assisted by Britain to develop into "bulwarks against Bolshevism in the East and West".

And then, inevitably, the wreckers inside the Soviet Union made a common front with Germany and Japan. The gigantic conspiracy is being unfolded in the present trial. The threads of the previous trials are being drawn together. No need here to amplify or explain the evidence – it speaks for itself.

The roots of the cancer are being ruthlessly plucked out. We must, however, appreciate one point clearly – there is a lot of talk about 'confessions' – it is not a question of confessions which bring to light the deeds of these criminals. These people have been forced to admissions when faced with the facts produced by the judicial authorities. They can no longer hide the truth.

You will remember how Zinoviev and Kamenev grovelled when faced with the death sentence and cried out that they had revealed everything. The facts show they had told nothing in comparison with what they were still hiding. The evidence of *Yagoda* is conclusive on this point. The full facts only come to light now through the patient and painstaking work of the Soviet authorities."[1]

Of course, any careful reading of the trial script would have shown that Bukharin made very few tangible specific "admissions" at all, and was confronted with no material evidence outside the "confessions" of others.[2] Indeed, at one point in his final plea, he insisted that "confessions are a medieval principle of jurisprudence".[3] What Bukharin did plead was his "guilt" in some overall moral-political sense, detached from any particular criminal action. It is nowadays widely believed that this abstract plea was the price of the lives of his young wife, Larina, and their baby son. But Pollitt had scarcely had time to familiarise himself with the trial record, since his copy had to be in *Inprecor* which actually appeared on the 19 March, only days after the conclusion of the event upon which he was commenting.

public trial leaves upon us the same impression, so far as concerns
the actual defendants, though without necessarily endorsing the
judgement on Trotsky himself, who was not before the Court, and
of whose personal participation there was little testimony that
would have been accepted as evidence in a British court . . . .

If we may attempt a detached and philosophical interpretation
of these proceedings, alike of the various defendants and of the
Government which brought them to trial and sentence – a hypo-
thetical explanation which is not offered as a justification of either
party – we suggest that they are the inevitable aftermath of any
long-drawn-out revolutionary struggle that ends in a successful
seizure of power. The successive generations of Russian revolutionaries, continuing for a whole century, during which they were
hunted by the Tsar's police, in constant peril of exile and imprisonment, flogging and death, were moulded to a particular "pattern of
behaviour" which became a fixed character. Lies and aliases, deceit
and trickery, theft and assassination, filled their whole lives. These
revolutionary conspirators, successive generations of whom we have
known personally in exile, were not criminals in the ordinary sense.
Even if it came to them in their warfare to commit theft, forgery or
murder, they cannot accurately be classed as thieves, forgers and
murderers. The best of them were heroic, even if we think them
mistaken; though some among them succumbed to the temptation
of betraying their comrades and even becoming tsarist spies and
agents provocateurs.

An analogous manifestation of the same pattern of behaviour
may be traced in the action of those who have come to the top, and
who are now concerned to "maintain the revolution". They are
incurably distrustful of the loyalty of their colleagues. Opposition,
however reasonably expressed, looks likes defeatism and incipient
rebellion. Every passing grumbling among the intelligentsia starts a
jealous watchfulness which goes far to make life intolerable. A
whole crop of suspicions, jealousies, delations, accusations and
counter-revolutionary struggle ending in a constitutional upheaval
as the subsequent conspiracies and attempts at counter-revolution
themselves . . . .

Now to get back to the Russian conspirators who have, during
the decade 1927-1937, been convicted on their own confessions of
attempts to create a counter-revolution. Are not such attempts at a
counter-revolution exactly what was to be expected? Has there ever
been a great and successful revolution without attempts at a counter-
revolution? The Stalin group, who now constitute the government,
have had immense difficulties to face in their fight against famine,
and in their effort to raise to a higher level of efficiency and civilisation what is reputed to have been the worst peasantry in the world.

In establishing the new social order it was inevitable that there
should arise, throughout the whole decade, honest and legitimate
differences of opinion as to policy. What were those differences? We

need not recite here the earlier issues on which, between 1921 and 1927, Trotsky and his shifting groups of friends took one view, whilst Stalin and his following took another . . . .

How long is this apparently continuous series of conspiracies and attempts at counter-revolutions likely to last? The only probably answer is that sporadic attempts of this kind – arising as they do fundamentally from the pattern of behaviour by which the lives of the conspirators have been moulded – may well continue as long as the pattern of behaviour itself. This, as experience indicates, is a lifelong matter. Not until the present generation of those whose early lives were spent in underground conspiracies against the Tsar has passed away will the USSR be as free from attempts at counter-revolution as Great Britain became after 1760, generations after the century of rebellions of 1641-1745. With the ever-increasing success of Soviet Communism in solving the paradox of poverty in the midst of plenty, which capitalism seems to find insoluble, these spasmodic attempts will become more feeble, and will be presently confined to incipient conspiracies which are strangled at birth by the public opinion of the rising generation. But the pattern of behaviour fades slowly in those whom it has moulded, and only with the death of the last of those who conspired against Nicholas and Stolypin will it have entirely disappeared. "For a long time to come", wrote Lenin to one of his followers in November 1922,* "there will be doubts, uncertainty suspicion and treachery", a forecast which is borne out by the evidence in the Moscow trials of 1937 . . . .

Possibly quite unconnected with such treasonable conspiracies as were widely suspected, was another series of trials in many of the constituent republics in the course of 1937 in which highly placed officials, mostly, but not exclusively, Party members, were found guilty of various forms of malversation, including embezzlement and diversion of public property to private uses, shameless extravagance and riotous living at the tax-payers' expense, coupled with forgery and fraudulent accountancy in some cases, and of culpable negligence, amounting to bribery and connivance, and positive wrecking, in others. That many cases of this kind should occur in a population now risen to 180 millions must be regarded as inevitable . . . The occurence within a year of a few hundred cases of administrative corruption, whether in the federal republic or municipal enterprises, or in the co-operative or trade union movements, in a community having four times the population of Britain or France and one-third more than that of the United States, would not in these countries seem in any way remarkable."[13]

In the same vein, John Strachey was to write:

"I believe that the psychological student of the future will look

*The Letters of Lenin, translated and edited by Elizabeth Hill and Doris Mudie, 1937, p.475.

back on the long-drawn-out incredulity of British public opinion
over the Moscow trials as one of the strangest . . . phenomena."

His biographer goes on to record:

"He then went on to dismiss as the height of implausibility the
suggestions that the defendants in these trials confessed because
their lives, or the lives of their wives and children, were spared;
though these were, indeed, the main reasons for the confessions."[14]

By contrast, since 1956, some prominent Western
Communists have already made clear and sometimes
moving statements repudiating their witness of the 'thirties.
Foremost among these is perhaps Ernst Fischer, the Austrian
marxist writer, who wrote a heartbreakingly honest account
of his unwitting complicity in what he later came to regard
as judicial murder.[15]

He found himself at the second trial, sitting by Feuchtwanger, who was about to become the author of the most
sycophantic of all the books to be published on the purges.

"Next to me sat a small man with a look of thoughtful concentration
on his exceptionally intelligent and likeable face: Lion Feuchtwanger. I had not met him before. He turned to me:
    'What do you make of it?'
    'As a non-Communist you're more impartial than I am. What do
you make of it?'
    'I followed the Zinoviev and Kamenev trial at a distance, in the
West. What I read in the papers seemed highly implausible. One
simply couldn't believe it. But here at close quarters, in the atmosphere of Moscow, where one can see and hear everything . . .'
    Feuchtwanger went on thoughtfully: 'The first trial reminded
me of some gruesome play. But this trial . . . the impression it
makes on the senses is wholly convincing. If this is a fabrication,
then I don't know what's genuine . . .'
    'So you believe the confessions . . .?'
    'To be genuine. I can see no other alternative. The indictment is
open to question. But the accused carry conviction. One only has
to observe their relaxed movements, their dispassionate, natural way
of discussing things. If it were a masquerade it would have needed
years of rehearsal and even then it would never have looked as
uncontrived as this. What convinces more than anything else is the
manner, the intonation, the attitude of the accused. That could
never get across in a transcript of the proceedings. I daresay that
many of my friends, if they simply read the transcript, will find this
trial as abhorrent as the first; I myself, having laid a finger in the

wound, know that it isn't an illusion. There is much that is obscure, inexplicable – but the alternative is utterly unthinkable.'

So it was; Feuchtwanger's view does not excuse the obfuscation of my consciousness but for me, too, the alternative was unthinkable. And, indeed, it still is, although we now know that the unthinkable actually happened. At the time I asked myself whether it was conceivable that the Soviet Union should be in a highly critical situation, that her economy should be lagging behind both plans and requirements, that the old Bolsheviks should be sacrificing themselves and taking the blame so as to save what had been achieved in October 1917 and was now in jeopardy. In themselves these things were not, I thought, inconceivable. But then the old Bolsheviks would surely have preserved their dignity, would not have accused themselves of the most infamous crimes, would not have showered accusations on the expatriate Trotsky. This alternative must therefore be excluded. But I did not, dared not, entertain the notion that the trial had been instigated by Stalin, that he was the murderer of Kirov and that it was he who was responsible for the disgrace, the destruction, the annihilation of the old Bolsheviks, of virtually all Lenin's comrades-in-arms. To me that was something utterly unthinkable."

So wide a controversy still has its reverberations four decades later on: what this small selection from a large contemporary library which includes a great deal of tendentious and untrue reportage does show is that there is no way in which the Bukharin and related cases may be regarded as simply the property of the Soviet authorities.

Regrettably, so much of the energy of a world-wide socialist movement was expended in establishing the case against Bukharin that this whole infamous business has become to some degree a world-wide responsibility. Truly, the onus is on the Soviet Communists to initiate restitution, and were they so to do, others might be relieved to allow them to sort things out. But all those who have inherited a share, however small, in the responsibility, must feel it their duty to press for some beginning to that necessary revaluation.

FOOTNOTES

1. Pollitt: *The Crushing of the Traitors – a Triumph for Peace and Socialism:* International Press Correspondence, No.14, 19 March 1938, p.309 *et seq.* A similar view was put forward in a British Communist Party pamphlet published in May

1938: R. Page Arnot and Tim Buck: *Fascist Agents Exposed in the Moscow Trials.* Tim Buck was, of course, spokesman of the Canadian Communists.

2.   Cf, notably Katkov: *The Trial of Bukharin,* London, Batsford, 1969; and Stephen F. Cohen's exhaustively comprehensive biography: *Bukharin and the Bolshevik Revolution,* London, Wildwood House, 1974. Fitzroy Maclean, who attended the trial, gives an eyewitness account which emphasises this view in *Eastern Approaches,* London, Pan Books, 1956, pp.55 *et.seq.*

3.   *Report of Court Proceedings,* p.778.

4.   Pollitt, *op.cit.,* p.309, col.II.

5.   Khrushchev, *op.cit.,* p.352.

6.   *The Communist International,* Vol.XIII, No.10, Nov-Dec 1936, p.641.

7.   M. Ercoli *The Lessons of the Trial of the Trotsky-Zinovievist Terrorist Centre,* Communist International, XIII, 10, pp.341-51.

8.   Togliatti: *Answers to Nine Questions.* In C. Wright Mills, *The Marxists,* London, Penguin Books, 1963, pp.372-3.

9.   E.g., article in *News Chronicle: The Moscow Trial Was Fair,* reprinted in 'Russia Today' pamphlet, n.d. (1936?) and foreword to *Soviet Justice at the Trial of Radek and Others,* by Dudley Collard: Left Book Club (Gollancz) 1937.

10.   *Autobiography of D.N. Pritt:* Vol.1, From Right to Left. London, Lawrence and Wishart, 1965, p.112. Pritt has the gall to continue ". . . industrious anti-Soviet propagandists in the West — those who sought to find a basis for their stories instead of just inventing them — eagerly studied the transcript, believed they had found a certain number of errors of fact in it which would help discredit the trial, and published the errors broadcast. I and others then, naturally, studied the allegations, and found that they were not in fact errors, although they looked as if they might be". (p.113).

11.   *The Second World War:* I. 1948, London, Cassell, pp.288-9.

12.   Cited in Sayers and Kahn: *The Great Conspiracy,* New York, Boni and Caer, pp.111 *et seq.* It should be mentioned that this work is a particularly offensive by-product of the Soviet purge industry.

13.   *Op.cit.,* pp.926 *et seq.* The Webbs' support for the Purges may be understood more fully in the light of the Correspondence, edited by Norman Mackenzie, and published by Cambridge University Press in 1978. (See especially Volume III). For a comprehensive discussion of pathetic literature on this matter, see David Caute: *The Fellow Travellers,* London, Quartet, 1977.

14.   Hugh Thomas: *John Strachey,* Eyre Methuen, 1973, p.164.

15.   *An Opposing Man,* London, Allen Lane, the Penguin Press, 1974, pp.304 *et seq.*

N.I. Bukharin.

CHAPTER V

Some Other Light on Bukharin

Bukharin had not always been valued so little. The impression he made on foreign socialists when they had been able to meet him on equal terms was very different:

"I first saw Bukharin in Vienna in the winter of 1913-14, at one of those arrangements common in the Russian colonies abroad, literary and political lectures, discussions, occasionally even dances. There used to be quite a few striking faces in the audience, even Trotsky was sometimes present at those gatherings. But Bukharin stood out among them through a quality of his own. There was in his appearance something of a saint, rather than a rebel or a thinker. The image of Count Myshikin of Dostoyevsky's *Idiot* involuntarily sprang to mind, at least the way the Russian actors tried to portray him. Perhaps this made me detect at once the mainly humanitarian aspect of that unusual man."

This was the view of the German Communist, Rosa Meyer-Levine.[1] Joseph Berger, one-time secretary of the Palestine Communist Party, describes him in more prosaic terms:

"If Lenin represented the first revolutionary generation of Bolsheviks and Trotsky the second, Bukharin belonged to the third – he was only in his thirties when I first met him. Of all the Politbureau, he had been the one who disagreed and argued with Lenin most often. They complemented each other, and their differences gave life and movement to the intellectual leadership. But he regarded himself as Lenin's pupil and imitated his manners, his resolute air and his crisp, dramatically simple way of expressing himself. It was the fashion, set by Lenin, to reduce the most involved political and philosophical notions to the simplest formulas. However, Bukharin's ideas were less clear cut, he was less shrewdly aware of their practical implications, and he relied more on brilliance of style.

It was said afterwards, when the hunt was up, that he was too dogmatic. His books may support this view, but in conversation he was warm, flexible and impressionable. He digressed freely, and you could feel that he was talking partly to make up his own mind. He was interested in what other people had to say. He drew out his subordinates, and never let them feel snubbed when a decision went against them. He surrounded himself with young people and students. They liked him and he influenced their ideas (for a time this was useful to Stalin, who had none of his expansive charm)."[2]

During the chaotic revolutionary days, the English journalist, Arthur Ransome, met many of the revolutionary leaders frequently, and was able to form characteristically clear-headed and liberal judgements about them. In 1919 he wrote a vivid description of Bukharin as he then was:

"Bukharin, member of the old economic mission to Berlin, violent opponent of the Brest peace, editor of *Pravda,* author of many books on economics and revolution, indefatigable theorist, found me drinking tea at a table in the Metropole.

I had just bought a copy of a magazine which contained a map of the world, in which most of Europe was coloured red or pink for actual or potential revolution. I showed it to Bukharin and said, "You cannot be surprised that people abroad talk of you as of the new Imperialists".

Bukharin took the map and looked at it.

"Idiotism, rank idiotism!" he said. "At the same time", he added, "I do think we have entered upon a period of revolution which may last fifty years before the revolution is at last victorious in all Europe and finally in all the world".

Now, I have a stock theory which I am used to set before revolutionaries of all kinds, nearly always with interesting results. I tried it on Bukharin. I said:

"You people are always saying that there will be revolution in England. Has it not occurred to you that England is a factory and not a granary, so that in the event of revolution we should be immediately cut off from all food supplies? According to your own theories, English capital would unite with American in ensuring that within six weeks the revolution had nothing to eat. England is not a country like Russia, where you can feed yourselves somehow or other by simply walking to where there is food. Six weeks would see starvation and reaction in England. I am inclined to think that a revolution in England would do Russia more harm than good."

Bukharin laughed. "You old counter-revolutionary!" he said. "That would be all true, but you must look further. You are right in one thing. If the revolution spreads in Europe, America will cut off food supplies. But by that time we shall be getting food from Siberia".

"And is the poor Siberian railway to feed Russia, Germany, and England?"

"Before then Pichon and his friends will have gone. There will be France to feed too. But you must not forget that there are the cornfields of Hungary and Roumania. Once civil war ends in Europe, Europe can feed herself. With English and German engineering assistance we shall soon turn Russia into an effective grain supply for all the working men's republics of the Continent. But even then the task will be only beginning. The moment there is revolution in England, the English-colonies will throw themselves eagerly into the arms of America. Then will come America's turn, and, finally, it is quite likely that we shall all have to combine to overthrow the last stronghold of capitalism to some South African bourgeois republic. I can well imagine", he said, looking far away with his bright little eyes through the walls of the dark dining room, "that the working men's republics of Europe may have to have a colonial policy of an inverse kind. Just as now you conquer backward races in order to exploit them, so in the future you may have to conquer the colonists to take from them the means of exploitation. There is only one thing I am afraid of."

"And what is that?"

"Sometimes I am afraid that the struggle will be so bitter and so long drawn out that the whole of European culture may be trampled under foot" . . . I finished my tea in silence. Bukharin, after carelessly opening these colossal perspectives, drank his tea in one gulp, prodigiously sweetened with my saccharin, reminded me of his illness in the summer, when Radek scoured the town for sweets for him, curing him with no other medicine, and then hurried off, fastening his coat as he went, a queer little De Quincey of revolution, to disappear into the dusk, before, half running, half walking, as his way is, he reached the other end of the big dimly lit, smoke-filled dining-room."[3]

Soon the passion subsided, and the revolution had more sombre perspectives to face. Bukharin became insistently concerned with the fear that "European culture" was losing ground in the new Soviet Union. More and more frequently he was compelled to defend freedom of expression against attacks by his own comrades.

Nadezhda Mandelstam, in her poignant memoir, describes the fury with which Bukharin greeted the news of her husband's uncomfortable interview with a Chekhist who was interrogating his arrested brother, back in 1922. She records the fact that Bukharin's intervention secured the victim's release, although she suspected his anger to be more the result of exasperation at inefficiency than resentment of the terror. But she also shows how the atmosphere changed, as Stalin's power was consolidated. Bukharin, she writes

"had always been a man of passionate temperament, quick to anger, but his way of venting his indignation changed with the times. Until 1928 he would just shout 'Idiots!' and pick up the phone, but after 1930 he just frowned and said: 'We must think whom to approach'."[3]

For all this enforced circumspection, Mandelstam's devoted widow never doubts Bukharin's loyalty to the virtue he had recognised in her husband. She imagines him, dead, ringing up to nag about the long delay in publishing those haunting poems.

In the event, much of Mandelstam's work found modern Soviet publishers long before Bukharin's own books could even be mentioned in print. Only for those outside the USSR, does the evidence of this extensive writing remain available to show that Bukharin was a humane man. He was also in many ways a compassionate one, and the vast literature of emigration contains many instances of his personal decency.

This was reflected in his political influence. After all, Lenin's own "testament" describes him as "the Party's rightful favourite", even if it also contains a schoolmasterly admonishment about his failure to master the dialectic, while praising his work as the "Party's most eminent and valuable theoretician". An alpha minus from Lenin was a good deal more than most people got, and Stalin, it will be remembered, received in the same document an unambiguous delta.[4]

In 1927, the Granat encyclopaedia published a series of autobiographies of the leading Bolsheviks, and something of Bukharin's engaging warmth can be seen in his contribution:

"When I was roughly five years old, my father was appointed tax inspector in Bessarabia. We lived there for approximately four years. Spiritually speaking, this period in my life was one of impoverishment. There were no books and the general atmosphere was typical of an outlying provincial town with all its charms. My younger brother and I were now a good deal freer from systematic education and spent much of our time outdoors. We grew up in gardens and fields, knew literally every tarantula hole in the garden, hunted death's-head butterflies, caught ground-squirrels, and so on. My greatest dream at the time was to be given the *Atlas of the Butterflies of Europe and the Central Asian Territories* and other similar works by Devrien. Then we moved back to Moscow and my father was without a job for two years. We lived in great poverty. I often collected bones and bottles to sell for two or three kopecks, and I would carry old newspapers round to the shop on the corner for half a kopeck. It was at this time that I entered the second form of the municipal primary school.

Although my father led a very dissolute life, he had an excellent knowledge of Russian literature, and among foreign writers held Heine in greatest esteem. At that time I read absolutely everything. I could recite pages of Heine and I knew the whole of Kuzma Prutkov by heart. I read all the classics whilst still very young."[5]

In the same brief autobiography, Bukharin adds:

"Of the most important stages of my political career, I consider it necessary to mention the Brest-Litovsk period when, at the head of the 'left communists', I made a colossal political blunder. The feature of the whole of the ensuing period was Lenin's growing influence on me, and I am indebted to him as to no other person for my Marxist education. Indeed, I was fortunate enough to be not only on the same side as him, but to be close to him both as a comrade and as a man."[6]

It is clear that Bukharin's devotion to Lenin was completely unfeigned. There is an interesting witness on this matter. During 1936, Bukharin was sent abroad by the Central Committee of the CPSU, to negotiate for the purchase of the archives of the German Social Democratic Party, which contained a prodigious literature by and about Karl Marx. Hitler's assumption of power had forced the archive and its owners into exile. Bukharin, together with Adoratsky, then director of the Marx-Engels-Lenin Institute, and Arosev, of the Cultural Relations body, VOKS, came to Paris with an offer of 10 million francs for the material.

The person in charge of the archive was Boris Nicolaevsky, a distinguished Menshevik scholar, whose brother was married to the sister of Rykov, Bukharin's close colleague and co-thinker. After their meetings Nicolaevsky wrote a semi-fictional collage of some of Bukharin's private remarks and some information given by a French Communist activist, which was published under the title *Letter of an old Bolshevik.* Years later, when this was republished, its author, who had, in the interval featured in the Bukharin trial *in absentia,* gave a long interview about the letter's background, and reported directly on what had been said by Bukharin during their private conversations. This is very relevant to an understanding of Bukharin's attitude to Lenin.

His remarks about Lenin were particularly interesting, too, because Bukharin was so devoted to him. Even when he spoke about their disagreements . . . he did so in a tone of warmth and friendship.

This is what he told me about the final period of Lenin's illness. From various details in Bukharin's account, I gathered that he meant the early fall of 1922. "Lenin would summon me to come and see him", Bukharin said. "The doctors had forbidden him to speak lest he become upset. But when I arrived, he would immediately take me by the hand and lead me into the garden. He would begin to speak: 'They don't want me to think about this. They say that this upsets me. But why don't they understand that I have lived my whole life this way? If I cannot speak about this, I become more upset than when I do speak. I calm down when I am able to talk about these matters with people like you'."

I asked Bukharin what the conversations had been about. He replied that he and Lenin spoke mostly about "leaderology", as we called it − that is, the problem of succession, of who was fit to be leader of the Party after Lenin was gone. "This", said Bukharin, "is what worried and upset Lenin the most".

In this connection, he told me that the last articles of Lenin's, *Better Less but Better,* about co-operatives and so forth, were only part of what Lenin had planned to do. He had wanted to put out another series of approximately the same number of articles which would give a complete picture of the future policy to be pursued. This was his principal goal.

Lenin's testament consisted of two parts, a small part about the leaders, and a bigger one about policies. I asked Bukharin what the principle of Lenin's policy was. He said to me: "I have written two things about this policy, *The Road to Socialism and the Worker-Peasant Alliance* and *Lenin's Political Testament.* The first is a pamphlet, which came out in 1925, the second was published in 1929". Bukharin asked me, "Do you remember those pamphlets?" I replied, "I confess I don't at present remember *The Road to Socialism".*

"That is the more interesting one", he said. "When I wrote it, I included my conversations with Lenin about the articles already published and those not yet published. I tried in that pamphlet to keep to only what Lenin thought, to what he told me. Of course, they were not quotations; my understanding of what he meant was reflected in what I wrote. But it was my outline of Lenin's ideas as he expounded them to me. The main point of his testament was that it is possible to arrive at Socialism without applying more force against the peasantry". The question concerned, of course, the treatment of the peasantry, which constituted 80 per cent of the population of Russia. In the opinion of Lenin and of all Communists in general, it was possible to apply force against the peasantry at a given moment, yet this was not to be made a permanent method of treatment. This was the point of *The Road to Socialism.*

With *Lenin's Political Testament,* Bukharin said, it was a different matter. "There were big arguments about it, and I had to write only what Lenin had already published. It was fundamentally the same thing. But the first pamphlet went further and the ideas in it were more crystallised; it did not stop at what he had already written."[7]

It remains a matter of dispute among scholars whether in fact Bukharin's assumptions about the logic of Lenin's own policies were justified. It is not necessary to become involved in that argument, here: what Nicolaevsky reports does not have to be accepted as the last word on the Soviet economic debate. But it does give powerful testimony about the state of Bukharin's mind, and of his fidelity to what he regarded as Lenin's commitment.

Yet, once the nightmare of his trial was being prepared, he received notice that he would be charged with the poisonously false accusation that he had conspired to bring about Lenin's death. This manifestly cut him more than any of the other counts in an indictment which today smells like a veritable witch's stew.

So fraught were the times that Bukharin could not rely on the written word to record his reactions to this miasma. He drafted a letter "to a future generation of communist leaders" and asked his wife, Larina, to memorise it. She rehearsed it until she was word-perfect, and after the execution, when she was seized, she took it into prison in her head. Upon her release, she wrote it down and sent it to the Central Control Commission of the CPSU. It was not poignant enough to move the members of that impassive body:

I am leaving life. I am lowering my head not before the proletarian axe, which must be merciless but also virginal. I feel my helplessness before a hellish machine, which, probably by the use of medieval methods, has acquired gigantic power, fabricates organised slander, acts boldly and confidently.

Dzerzhinskii is gone; the remarkable traditions of the Chekha have gradually faded into the past, when the revolutionary idea guided all its actions, justified cruelty to enemies, guarded the state against any kind of counterrevolution. That is how the Chekha earned special confidence, special respect, authority and esteem. At present, most of the so-called organs of the NKVD are a degenerate organisation of bureaucrats, without ideas, rotten, well-paid, who use the Chekha's bygone authority to cater to Stalin's morbid suspiciousness (I fear to say more) in a scramble for rank and fame, concoting their slimy cases, not realising that they are at the same time destroying themselves – history does not put up with witnesses of foul deeds.

Any member of the Central Committee, any member of the Party can be rubbed out, turned into a traitor, terrorist, diversionist, spy, by these "wonder-working organs". If Stalin should ever get any doubts about himself, confirmation would instantly follow.

Storm clouds have risen over the Party. My one head, guilty of nothing, will drag down thousands of guitless heads. For an organisation must be created, a Bukharinite organisation, which is in reality not only nonexistent now, the seventh year that I have had not a shadow of disagreement with the Party, but was also nonexistent then, in the years of the right opposition. About the secret organisations of Riutin and Uglanov, I knew nothing. I expounded my views, together with Rykov and Tomskii, openly.

I have been in the Party since I was eighteen, and the purpose of my life has always been to fight for the interests of the working class, for the victory of socialism. These days the paper with the sacred name *Pravda* prints the filthiest lie, that I, Nikolai Bukharin, have wished to destroy the triumphs of October, to restore capitalism. That is unexampled insolence, that is a lie that could be equalled in insolence, in irresponsibility to the people, only by such a lie as this: it has been discovered that Nikolai Romanov devoted his whole life to the struggle against capitalism and monarchy, to the struggle for the achievement of a proletarian revolution. If, more than once, I was mistaken about the methods of building socialism, let posterity judge me no more harshly than Vladmir Illich did. We were moving towards a single goal for the first time, on a still unblazed trail. Other times, other customs. *Pravda* carried a discussion page, everyone argued, searched for ways and means, quarrelled and made up and moved on together.

I appeal to you, a future generation of Party leaders, whose historical mission will include the obligation to take apart the monstrous cloud of crimes that is growing ever hungrier in these frightful times, taking fire like a flame and suffocating the Party.

I appeal to all Party members! In these days, perhaps the last of my life, I am confident that sooner or later the filter of history will inevitably sweep the filth from my head. I was never a traitor; without hesitation I would have given my life for Lenin's, I loved Kirov, started nothing against Stalin. I ask a new young and honest generation of Party leaders to read my letter at a Party Plenum, to exonerate me, and to reinstate me in the Party.

Know, comrades, that on that banner, which you will be carrying in the victorious march to communism, is also my drop of blood.

N. Bukharin[8]

It was this letter which provided the last sentence of Larin's 1978 appeal.

FOOTNOTES

1. From a memoir cited in Tarbuck (ed) *Imperialism and the Accumulation of Capital.* Allen Lane, The Penguin Press, 1972, p.8.
2. *Shipwreck of a Generation,* Harvill, 1971, pp.99-100. This book contains a graphic description of Bukharin's intervention at the 1934 Writers' Congress, the details of which are currently the subject of dispute among independent Soviet scholars.
3. *Hope Against Hope.* Collins, 1971, pp.114 *et seq.*
4. "Bukharin and Piatakov . . . are in my opinion, the most able forces (among the youngest) and in regard to them it is necessary to bear in mind the following: Bukharin is not only the most valuable and biggest theoretician in the Party, but also may legitimately be considered the favourite of the whole Party;" only after this does Lenin take leave to doubt whether Bukharin has "ever fully understood" the dialectic. Stalin, by contrast, "is too rude . . . I propose . . . to find a way to remove Stalin . . . and to appoint . . . another man who in all respects differs from Stalin only in superiority: namely, more patient, more loyal, polite and more attentive to comrades, less capricious, etc. . . ."
5. Cf. Georges Haupt and Jean-Jacques Marie, *Makers of the Russian Revolution.* Allen and Unwin, 1974.
6. *Ibid.,* p.34.
7. Nicolaevsky: *Power and The Soviet Elite.* Ann Arbor, 1975, pp.11-13.
8. This letter is reproduced from Roy Medvedev's *Let History Judge,* pp.183-4. If there is one indispensible book on the whole background to this case, this is it. Amongst other things, it points out some of the errors in Bukharin's own assumptions in this moving document.

"IT'S QUEER HOW YOU REMIND ME OF SOMEONE, JOSEF . . ."

CHAPTER VI

Bukharin's Constitution?

At the Seventh Congress of Soviets, in 1935, Molotov proposed a sweeping electoral reform, which would abolish open (public) voting by instituting a secret ballot, equalise the franchise and accord it to all citizens, and introduce direct elections. The Congress thereupon sanctioned the establishment of a Constitutional Commission, which was to be appointed by its Central Executive. This soon started work. Stalin was designated chairman, and in all 31 members were appointed. These included seven Presidents of the Union Republics, and also Kaganovitch, Molotov, Litvinov, Radek, Bukharin and Yakovlev. The last three of these perished in the purges, in spite of the guarantees which their subsequent Constitution offered, of "the inviolability of the person".

The draft which was prepared by this Commission was, according to the official biography of Stalin

"thrown open for nationwide discussion, which continued for five and a half months. There was not a corner in the country where this greatest document in human history was not studied and discussed. The draft Constitution was received with great joy by the whole Soviet people."[1]

The same biography, which Khrushchev was later to inform us had been written by a commission, but improved by its subject personally, (who found it necessary to add a liberal seasoning of praise for Stalin)[2] continues:

"The new Constitution was approved and adopted by the Eighth Congress of Soviets on December 5th 1936. It is unanimously called by the peoples of the USSR after its author – Stalin."[3]

Although it seems quite believable that Stalin did in fact compose this last sentence himself, it is clear that what he did *not* write was the Soviet Constitution of 1936. Roy

Medvedev specifically mentions Bukharin and Yakovlev among the true authors.[4] Nicolaevsky offers us an anecdote, which, if it is true, gives us a truly fascinating paradox:

"It was already clear from various signs that Bukharin had played a major role in drawing up the Constitution. He was secretary of the commission that worked out the draft Constitution. Back in 1930, he had come out with a draft for universal suffrage and fought for the elimination of all special privileges for the Communist Party, two points that were reflected in this Constitution. In addition, in his talk with me about the group of Gorky, Pavlov, and others, Bukharin gave the impression that the idea of the Constitution had originated with them.

Then, one day, while we were discussing "proletarian humanism", Bukharin took his fountain pen from his pocket and, showing it to me, he said: "Look carefully. With this, the entire new Soviet Constitution was written, from first word to last. And I bore the work alone; only Karlyusha (Radek) helped a little. I could come to Paris only because I had completed this work. All of the important decisions have already been taken. Now they are printing the text. And in this Constitution the people will have more room. They can no longer be pushed aside!"

Bukharin was very proud of this Constitution. Not only did it introduce universal and equal suffrage, it also established the equality of all citizens before the law. In general, it was a well-thought-out framework for the peaceful transition of the country from the dictatorship of one party to a genuine people's democracy. Bukharin said that the commission for drawing up the Constitution had even raised the question of having several candidates compete at elections."[5]

Sidney and Beatrice Webb celebrated this Constitution with a veritable panegyric, in their book on *Soviet Communism*. It was compared with both the Declaration of Rights of 1776, and the French revolutionary declaration of 1793, to their detriment, since, unlike the good utilitarians of Moscow, the great American and French founding fathers had omitted any mention of the *"duties of man"*. These, however, were somewhat amply itemised in the Soviet document. It is less than completely clear that this would have been welcomed by the author of the *Critique of the Gotha Programme*. The fact remains, however, whatever Bukharin's intention, that his Constitution, if indeed it was his, proved less than equal to the safeguarding of his own freedom from arbitrary arrest, to say nothing of the inviolability of the very many thousands of persons who perished in the storms of bloodlust which accompanied his downfall.

Even so, Bukharin has not left an empty legacy. The cry of a whole new generation of critics of the Soviet Establishment since 1956, has been, not "overthrow the Constitution" but "enforce the Constitution". Under this remarkable document, "secrecy of correspondence is guaranteed by law". So are freedom of speech, assembly and demonstration. It was in a context of mounting controversy about the non-implementation and violation of these provisions of the 1936 Constitution that the present Soviet Government launched the discussion about the new, 1977 Constitution. The revised document carries forward, almost unaltered, many of the key Bukharinian commitments of the older one. This is not the place in which to discuss the significance of the changes which have been made between the two versions. But it is appropriate to note at least one of the remarks made by Leonid Brezhnev when he presented the 1977 draft for ratification by the Supreme Soviet:

"Altogether some 400,000 proposals for amendments to individual articles have been made for the purpose of clarifying, improving and supplementing the wording of the Draft. Having made a careful study of these proposals – many of which, of course, recur – the Constitution Commission recommends that 110 articles of the Draft should be amended and one new article added."[6]

Even allowing for recurring proposals, a formidable process of compositing would be required to boil 400,000 amendments into a total of 111, and it would have been genuinely interesting to have seen a full and free debate on how this should be done. Unfortunately, to an outsider, all this does look like a highly controlled and manipulated process, one quite out of keeping with a situation in which

"the whole Soviet people . . . have in fact become the true creators of the Fundamental Law of their State."[7]

as Mr Brezhnev puts it.

In fact the level of public controversy which could be expected to be generated in a real debate on a Constitution for socialist democracy seems to have been conspicuously missing in this particular debate. No one need doubt that "over 450,000 open Party meetings were held for this purpose" nor that "these were addressed by more than three million men and women". These statistics would have much impressed the Webbs, who would also have favoured the apparent unanimity which accompanied them.

We find one statistic more impressive still, however: the man who was certainly at least a co-author, probably the key contributor, and possibly the sole author of the out-going Constitution, remains the victim of a nightmare official conspiracy which did not spare him the duty of accepting the most humiliating and demeaning slanders before it had him shot. This statistic: one death, over-shadows all past and present Soviet Constitutions until they can find a means to permit the truth to be told about it. Legions of other victims still need redress. This one, though, is special. How can Law possibly prevail in a State which cannot secure justice even for its author?

FOOTNOTES

1. G.F. Alexandrov *et al: Joseph Stalin: A Short Biography,* Moscow, FLPH 1949, p.132. In fact, Human History might, if ransacked, offer perhaps one or two further documents which most of us would be happy to rank not too far below this one.
2. N.S. Khrushchev: *The Secret Speech,* Spokesman, 1976, p.67, *et seq.*
3. Alexandrov, *op.cit.,* p.134.
4. *Let History Judge,* p.512.
5. Boris Nicolaevsky: *Power and the Soviet Elite.* Ann Arbor, p.22.
6. Leonid Brezhnev: Report on the Draft Constitution (October 4th 1977) *International Affairs,* Moscow, p.4.
7. *Ibid.*

Stalin's statue at Yerevan, Armenia.

CHAPTER VII

Securing Redress

When the Russell Foundation received Yuri Larin's appeal, we were aware that distinguished partisans of the European Communist movement had already expressed disquiet about his father's case. Jean Ellenstein, the French Communist historian, in his *The Stalin Phenomenon,* comments adversely on the Moscow trials, and this book has been widely circulated among the French left. Paolo Spriano, in the third volume of his *Storia del Partito Comunista Italiano,* which is virtually the official history of the PCI, also criticises the trials strongly. Santiago Carrillo, in *Eurocommunism and the State,* reveals a keen appreciation of the effects of Stalinism on Soviet institutions. On a different level of political influence, the British communists had, only in March 1978, published a column specifically in memory of Bukharin in their monthly periodical, *Marxism Today.*

"Last month (March) saw the fortieth anniversary of the death of Nikolai Ivanovich Bukharin. Born in 1888 Bukharin joined the Bolshevik Party in 1906. Both a theorist and an organiser, he was elected to its Central Committee in July 1917, and in October-November became one of the leaders of the Moscow uprising. He was appointed editor of *Pravda* in December 1917, and held this post until 1929. For a brief period in the middle twenties, after the death of Lenin but before Stalin emerged as a sole leader, Bukharin reached the summit of authority as a Bolshevik. Between 1926 and 1929 he also headed the Communist International. For thirty years until his arrest in 1937 he was one of the outstanding figures of Soviet Marxism . . ."

After recording the story of Bukharin's execution, the article went on:

"Revelations since 1955 about the criminality prevalent in judicial processes in the Stalin period threw doubt on this verdict. It would be an exaggeration to say that his case was reopened, and in Soviet terms Bukharin remains on the whole an 'unperson'. But his guilt was no more proven than that of many others who suffered repression and were later exonerated, and in the early 1960s several historians and political figures spoke out for Bukharin's innocence.

From an historical standpoint Bukharin's role and significance have always seemed overshadowed by others. Despite a brief involvement with the Left Communists during and at the end of the Civil War, Bukharin never became a major faction leader like Kamenev and Zinoviev. On the contrary he was for many years a leader of the whole party. When he fell into disagreement with official attitudes, he played out his opposition from within the Central Committee, avoiding the role which fell to Trotsky of criticism from without. Compared with Stalin he based his politics not on militancy, shock troops and grandiose plans, but on organising the step-by-step transformation of Soviet culture from below. Many of his ideas bore similarity with those of Gramsci."[1]

Valuable as these statements were, they were not direct responses to Larin's appeal. They did not necessarily carry the full political weight of their Parties behind them, and they were not addressed to the Soviet authorities, who alone had it in their power to give sadly inadequate redress to the Larin family.

After consultation, we therefore decided to circulate Larin's letter to Berlinguer for information, and to request a wide cross-section of public figures in the various socialist and communist parties among whom we were known to endorse an appeal to Mr Brezhnev. At the beginning, since it was not our intention to "pressurise" Mr Berlinguer, we asked all recipients of our letter to respect its confidentiality until the Italian Communists had had the opportunity to make their own response. Although we wrote to dozens of people, and received support from a whole cross-section of the socialist movement, not one of the many who received this appeal broke the confidence.

The reply from the Italian Communists, when it came, was dramatic and completely unambiguous. On Friday, June 16th the Party newspaper, *Unita* published a long statement by Paolo Spriano, (who had already privately endorsed the appeal) which we reproduce as an appendix to this booklet. It began with the injunction "the need to do justice to this eminent representative of the international communist movement, as well as to the other victims of the trials of the '30s, is not merely a problem concerning their historical merit, but a moral and political necessity."

A week later, the text of the Larin letter was published in the independent newspaper, *La Repubblica*,[2] together with another strong interview with Spriano, and a statement from Aldo Tortorella, the PCI's main official spokesman on cultural affairs. Subsequently, *Rinascita,* the Party's cultural weekly, featured a long article.[3] Meantime, the signatures to the appeal were flooding in: French Communists Althusser and Balibar, the international secretary of the French Socialists, Robert Pontillon, Claude Bourdet of the radical Unified Socialist Party, and Simone de Beauvoir; the secretary of the Greek Communists, the Spanish historian Claudin, and the leader of the Fourth International Ernest Mandel; from the USA, Noam Chomsky, Corliss Lamont, Joe Hansen and Robert Cohen, Bukharin's biographer; the Australian Communist Party, which sent a heartwarming letter of complete solidarity: and Pierre Joye, the veteran Belgian Communist leader.

In England, a number of Labour MPs and several members of the Party Executive endorsed the appeal. The Labour Party newspaper, *Labour Weekly,* carried a full report:

A worldwide campaign has been launched on behalf of a long-dead victim of the Stalin purges.

Labour MPs have joined socialists in 15 countries to urge the Soviet Union to rehabilitate Nikolai Bukharin, the leading Kremlin theorist after Lenin's death, who was executed after a show trial in 1938 . . .

In Britain it is backed by Labour Party chairman Joan Lestor and seven other Labour MPs – Ian Mikardo, Norman Buchan, Geoff Edge, Martin Flannery, Eric Heffer, Stan Newens and Audrey Wise. Playwrights Tom Stoppard, Trevor Griffiths and Howard Brenton, and members of the Bertrand Russell Peace Foundation which is co-ordinating the British appeal, are also among those who have signed.

They are demanding that the Soviet Union give a "full explanation to the circumstances which led to Bukharin's wrongful conviction . . ."

Liverpool Walton MP Eric Heffer, who has signed the appeal, says: "Undoubtedly the charges against him were part and parcel of Stalinism.

"If the Soviet Union is to get back to a democratic type of regime, which it had for only a short time after the revolution, it will have to accept that there were fundamentally vicious policies which they will have to totally repudiate.

"Bukharin was a great political leader and one of the early Bolsheviks, a man of tremendous intellectual ability"."[4]

We discovered that a play had been written on the Bukharin trial by Andy McSmith, and was scheduled to be premiered at the Royal Court Theatre in August 1978. Both playwright and theatre agreed to help in the campaign. We also learned that a scholarly symposium on Bukharin's work was in preparation, and we decided to continue to collect further signatures to the appeal until that took place.

Meantime, the first batch of signatures have been sent forward to the Soviet authorities, and we await their reply.

FOOTNOTES

1. *Editorial Comments,* pp.99-100.
2. *La Repubblica,* 22nd June 1978, p.12.
3. *I Conti con tutto il nostro passato,* by Guiliano Procacci: Rinascita, No.26, 30th June 1978, pp.23-4.
4. Harold Frayman: *Appeal for Victim of Stalinism, Labour Weekly,* 30th June, 1978.

Appendix I

Old Bolsheviks Appeal

After the XXIInd Party Congress, four old Party activists[1] sent the following letter to the Politburo:

"Dear Comrades, Members of the Presidium of the Central Committee (i.e. the Politburo):

We appeal to you on an important matter. The path of the Bolshevik revolutionary N.I. Bukharin, stretching over thirty years, was complex. On that path he committed serious mistakes of a theoretical and political order, for which he caught it from Lenin more than once. But Lenin's criticism of Bukharin's mistakes never questioned his devotion to the Party and the Revolution: that was criticism and arguments with *a man who shared his views on the basic problems of Bolshevism.*

N. Bukharin was noted for his ability to admit his mistakes and correct them without false pride. For that very reason in Lenin's time he not put out of the Party for his mistakes; he was a member of the Politburo and for twelve years the editor of the central organ, *Pravda.*

In his Testament, giving as it were final characteristics of some Party officials, a stocktaking of the entire past, Lenin called Bukharin *the biggest and the most valuable theorist in the Party.*

Bukharin was expelled from the Party and removed from the Central Committee only in 1937, on the basis of testimony given during the 'investigation' of his alleged espionage and terrorist activity, the absurdity of which is now clear to everyone. P. Pospelov, a member of the Central Committee, at the All-Union Conference of Historians in December, 1962, declared unequivocally (and this was published in the press) that Bukharin was no terrorist or spy. How then, after such a definite declaration at a gathering of two thousand people and in the press, can one preserve the verdict of the court and the expulsion from the Party in the absence of a corpus delicti?

This discredits the court. And he was condemned and expelled from the Party not for mistakes on the problems of Brest or for disagreements over collectivisation.

Annulment of the illegal verdict and reinstatement of Bukharin in the Party will not only be acts to restore justice personally in relation to one of our Party's outstanding leaders of the Leninist period; they will also play a big role in the further elaboration of the

Party's history during the relevant periods, which is extremely hampered just now by the forbidden position of Bukharin's name: only bad things can be written about him now, which leads to distortion of these sections of history in general.

We think that restoration of the truth and annulment of decisions based on false documents will raise still higher our Party's authority and our country's prestige.

We, who knew Bukharin personally at many stages of our glorious history, with his shortcomings and his merits as a Bolshevik revolutionary, fully understand and share such warm words of Lenin, spoken by him in the last minutes of his life, as a sort of farewell to the Party, such words about Nikolai Bukharin as the *Testament* does not have concerning any one else: *the rightful favourite of the Party.*

Those words are a great obligation on all of us, and that forces us to turn to you, members of the Party Presidium, with the request not to let the name of a man who was so appreciated by Lenin remain in the camp of traitors, and to rehabilitate Bukharin from the charges made in 1937, by annulling the verdict and reinstating him in the Party.

A man whom Lenin called *the rightful favourite of the Party* cannot remain in the list of traitors and outcasts from the Party."

All four of the old Bolsheviks who signed this letter have died, and their appeal remains unanswered.

FOOTNOTE

1. E. Stasova, Party member since 1898; V. Karpinskii, member since 1898; P. Katanlan, member since 1903; and A. Rudenko, member since 1905. This letter is reproduced from *Let History Judge*, by Roy Medvedev.

Appendix II
Paolo Spriano :
The Bukharin Case

The need to do justice to the eminent representative of the international Communist movement, as well as to the other victims of the trials of the '30s, is not merely a problem concerning their historical merit, but a moral and political necessity.

Forty years have gone by since the tragic death of Nikolai Bukharin, the Bolshevik leader who Lenin called the Benjamin of the Party. *L'Unita* in a lengthy article (by Giuseppe Boffa on March 26th last) has already paid tribute to the person and experience of Bukharin, and to the value of his ideas.

But the question of the great historic silence which continues in the USSR, twenty-two years after the XXth Congress, about him as well as other major leaders who were accused and condemned in the 1936-38 Moscow Trials, is a question which still concerns us.

Bukharin's widow, and his son, Yuri Larin (Bukharin) who had only just been born at the time his father was shot, both spent years in a concentration camp, and have both, since their release, several times requested the Soviet authorities and the leadership of the Communist Party of the Soviet Union (CPSU) for the rehabilitation of their relative. Appeals in support of this action had been formulated in 1961, by some old Bolsheviks, including comrade Stasova, one-time secretary of Lenin and of the Comintern. It seemed as if, after the XXIInd Congress of the CPSU, in 1961, in which the Soviet leaders revealed, much more explicity than had been made plain earlier at the XXth Congress, the measure of the Stalinist repressions, (exercised both against the masses as well as against members of the Party and military and political leaders) seemed then as if Bukharin himself might be the first great victim of those trials whose reputation could have been officially freed from the monstrous accusations, formulated in 1938, of having been a spy of foreign secret services, a paid traitor, even of having conspired to kill Lenin. Those accusations, which were obviously false in addition to being infamous, had never been upheld by any confession of the defendant, who, in order to save his family, admitted to having been responsible for a "complex" conspiracy. But, in 1964, that page, not quite reopened, was soon firmly sealed down again. Now, on the 40th anniversary of Bukharin's death, his son has revived his appeal and the Bertrand Russell Peace Foundation has taken it up.

This we cannot ignore. Italian Communist scholars, the leading bodies of the Party, and its members, from 1956 up to the present day, have without reticence given their judgement on these and other pages of Soviet history, and of the history of world Communism, have defined aberrant judical enquiries, trials, condemnations, and repressions for what they truly were. Bukharin's role has been studied by us as one of the most interesting, not only within the contemporary marxist debate, but also in the heat of the choices and political decisions which had to be taken in the process of building a new society. This has not been in the past, and certainly is not now, a question of idealising his contribution. It is in truth a question of doing as Lenin and Gramsci did in their own time: of passionately discussing the theoretical and economic thought of Bukharin and of evaluating as a whole the effective part which Bukharin played in crucial moments of Soviet history: from the days which preceded the Revolution to the Brest-Litovsk peace, from the elaboration of NEP to the struggle fought with Stalin against the Left opposition in 1924-26, from the great debates about industrialisation and collectivisation of the country up to the dramatic squeeze of the internal struggle which preceded Stalin's absolute supremacy over both the Party and the State.

A series of studies and researches by Giuseppe Boffa, Ernesto Ragionieri, Guiliano Procacci and other comrades have all grappled with these problems.

It is evident that faced with Bukharin's contribution one is not simply confronted by the necessity — though sacrosanct — of a moral rehabilitation, because such a necessity is also valid for the other victims of those trials, for Zinoviev, and for Kamenev, for Piatakov and for Radek, for Rykov and for so many like them, covered with slanderous accusations and sentenced to direct execution or death by

attrition during imprisonment. A correct historic evaluation
of Bukharin's contribution involves those great themes
which, not by chance, were the first ones, after the XXth
Congress, to have re-opened by Soviet historians, linked to
the same development and to the new problems of the
USSR: questions of agricultural policy, of the methods and
costs of accumulation in the rural areas etc. The need for
further research and thought has anything but disappeared.
Every party and every people needs to be able to face freely
its own history without falling into Manichean attitudes or
pronouncing ostracisms. Facing the Stalinist era, with the
mistakes and deformations which were publicly denounced
by the highest leaders of the CPSU, is one of the conditions
for the renewal of the present Soviet society. For us as
well, to keep alive "The Case of Bukharin" has a general
significance which is of historic importance, as well as having
moral, theoretical, educational and political coherence.

To favour, in the spirit of the truth, a rational investigation of the events of the past is part of our struggle
against all forms of intolerance and dogmatism. The trage-
dies as well as the achivements of socialism, constitute a
pathway of experiences, positive and negative, which
must be put to use. Could we perhaps dismiss from our
elaboration the lessons which come from the past, from
the international working class movement? Certainly
not. In fact, our understanding of socialism, as the most
advanced and most just form of social organisation, which
strengthens itself and feeds on the defence and the expansion of democracy and lives concretely in the freedom of
every one and of each individual without exploitation or
oppression, has become more mature and aware precisely
through the lessons of history. On the other hand, dogmatism, the impossibility of critically analysing the present,
of fully understanding the means and needs of action, are
often a result of a denial of the values which past experience
offers.

*　　　　*　　　　*

The Bertrand Russell Peace Foundation has addressed an
appeal to some Italian scholars to support a request to the
Soviet Government and Communist Party from Bukharin's
son, Yuri, for the rehabilitation of his father, tried and
condemned to death in Moscow in 1938. Amongst other

comrades, Paolo Spriano, Giuliano Procacci and Giuseppe Boffa have accepted the invitation.

The Foundation's invitation was accompanied by an open letter from Bukharin's son to PCI General Secretary, Enrico Berlinguer.

In signing the appeal, comrades Spriano, Procacci and Boffa have reaffirmed the position already taken by the PCI on this question . . .

Appendix III

Interview in La Repubblica

Paolo Spriano and Aldo Tortorella explain the positions of the PCI. "If today we are fighting for Bukharin, tomorrow we shall fight for Trotsky."

"We are making this move because the freedom from the knots of dogma might benefit development towards a socialist society."

Rome: "We didn't wait until yesterday to throw light on Bukharin's personality: Giuseppe Boffa, for example, has written clearly about him, presenting him as a most prominent participant in the Bolshevik events, who played a leading role in a form of struggle with Stalin. I myself, in the third volume of my *History of the Italian Communist Party,* have written several chapters about the slanders of the Moscow Trials. It is clear, however, that an article by a communist historian, published with some prominence in *L'Unita,* isn't there simply at Paolo Spriano's whim."

It is in fact Paolo Spriano to whom we are listening. He is referring to his own decisive stand in favour of the rehabilitation of Nikolai Ivanovich Bukharin, which appeared last Friday on the third page of the Communist daily. The article was printed alongside the news that the son of the great Bolshevik shot by Stalin in 1938, Yuri Larin, (he was born two years before they killed his father, and given this artifical name because it was unbearable that in Stalin's USSR somebody should be called Bukharin) through the Bertrand Russell Peace Foundation of Nottingham, has written an open letter to Berlinguer asking him to take the initiative to encourage the Communist Party of the Soviet Union to conclude the necessary proceedings to rehabilitate his father. These started some time ago, but have been lost in obscure political bureaucratic meanders, a sort of Kafka trial in reverse. The letter, together with an appeal which says "I support the request of Yuri Larin Bukharin and I urge the Soviet Government to reopen the case of Bukharin" which Spriano and others have signed and sent back, has not only been sent to Berlinguer but also to Paolo Spriano, Giuliano Procacci, Giuseppe Boffa, and "I think", says the Communist historian, "Lelio Basso as well". As one can see, the reaction of the PCI hasn't been a silent one, and it has provoked the explosion of a case which is not only an historic and cultural one, but it is also essentially political. Up to the present day, the PCI had never taken a position in favour of the "major" victims of the Stalinist trials. What is moving it now? At a time when Santiago Carrillo has abolished the term "Leninism" is it, perhaps, a signal for the opening of a great debate (to which Berlinguer recently referred in Barcelona) about the ideal roots of the Italian Communist Party? Along with the necessity to do justice to a leader of the October Revolution on a humane and moral level, as well as a strictly political one, is there, as far as the PCI is concerned, a rethinking and an approach to its own thesis of a "revolution at a snail's pace?"

"This question", answers Spriano, "should not be addressed to me, but to the leaders of the Party. As far as I am concerned, however, I think the problem goes beyond the political beliefs of the defendants in 1937, and it is necessary to rehabilitate all of Stalin's victims, including Trotsky".

Wasn't Togliatti, however, in a sense, a Bukharinite?

"This is a point on which there has been much discussion. Ragionieri himself talks about it. Undoubtedly there was a collaboration. Togliatti was in the USSR in 1926, the year of Bukharin's greatest influence. He was, at that time, Stalin's ally against the forces of the left. Undoubtedly all Bukharin's ideas about "gradualism", about "intermediary phases" (amongst other things he anticipated non-socialist democratic popular revolutions), about the relationship between workers and peasants, must have had some influence on Togliatti. One must also recall that Togliatti died in 1964, and in 1967 one might have assumed that the process of rehabilitation was going to carry on".

In fact, explains Spriano, this course had been urged for the first time by Stasova, then nearly ninety (amongst other things she had been Lenin's secretary, and President of the International Red Aid) together with some other old

Bolsheviks after the XXIInd Congress, "in which the debate was not limited to the Khrushchev secret report on the 'Stalinist purges' as had happened in 1956 during the XXth Congress, but now personalities like Mikoyan and Khrushchev himself gave figures from the rostrum. Only recently out of concentration camp – after Stalin's death – Yuri Larin and his mother joined in the request, addressed to Khrushchev, to reopen the process of rehabilitation of Nikolai Ivanovich. Khrushchev seemed to have accepted: but then everything came to a sudden stop. In 1964, anyhow, he lost power . . ."

From 'historic' questions to those more sharply political. We questioned Aldo Tortorella, who is responsible for cultural affairs in the PCI. He immediately pointed out that "our position of critical analysis of the experience of socialist societies does not begin with our concern about the Bukharin case".

But, up to today, you both always concerned yourself with lesser persons, not great celebrities?

"Perhaps it has not always been known that we Italian Communists, in the historical studies inspired by the Party – have for a considerable time rejected the interpretation which was given of the condemnation (not only on a moral level) of the majority of the Bolshevik Old Guard.

Therefore, it wasn't yesterday that we began a labour aimed at penetrating deeply and understanding with clarity, exhaustively, the work of great Communist personalities such as Bukharin, Zinoviev, Kamenev, Trotsky, aimed also at demystifying the accusations of which they have been made targets."

This kind of operation is no longer considered "an interference" in the internal affairs of the USSR?

"One has to be careful. One can pose a method of discussion directed at purely instrumental aims. In such a case, this could be mistaken, more or less sincerely, as a form of interference. It is evident, then, that there are a lot of people who are not in the least interested in a debate aimed at freeing marxism from its dogmatic encrustations, for the pure and simple reason that they are enemies of every form of socialism as such. We and others, on the contrary, are moving so that the freedom from traps and knots of dogmatism might serve the cause of the struggle for the socialist transformation of society."

Is the PCI becoming Bukharinist?

"To refute an historic slander about Bukharin's personality and his role, doesn't automatically imply supporting the positions he had taken. Gramsci, for example, in his *Prison Notebooks* polemicises (even given the special language he had to use in those notes) about certain of Trotsky's positions, about what was happening under Stalin's control, and also about Bukharin's interpretations of Marxist theory. And more: about the whole question of the 'Two cultures', the proletarian as opposed to the bourgeois, there was a controversy between Lenin and Bukharin himself, even though Lenin considered Bukharin to be the cleaverest bolshevik theorist.

The stand of the latter was rather more dogmatic and in some aspects riskier than Lenin's. Gramsci's analysis in fact tries to free him from this kind of dogmatism, expressed for example in Bukharin's *Manual of Sociology*.

In conclusion, what is the political motivation which lies behind this clear stand of the PCI?

"I think we have to continue along the path which has made our Party a great one: that of relating to the new problems set by reality. This also implies an effort of rigorous fidelty to our own goals, and, at the same time, a continuous innovative ability."

Appendix IV

Preliminary Signatories

I appeal to the Soviet Government for the re-opening of the case of N.I. Bukharin, his rehabilitation, and a public explanation of the circumstances which led to his wrongful conviction.

Australia
Eric Aarons   ) On behalf of
Joe Palmada   ) the Nat. Exec.
Mavis Robertson) of the CPA.
Alastair Davidson

Austria
Dr Gunther Anders
Josef Cap
Harald Irnberger
Leopold Grunwald
Dr Georg Lowy
Les Mache
Dr Eduard Marz
Dr Theodor Prager

Belgium
Pierre Joye
Professor Marcel Liebman
Ernest Mandel

Czechoslovakia
Professor Eduard Goldstucker
Jiri Pelikan

France
Louis Althusser
Etienne R.J. Balibar
Simone de Beauvoir
Claude Bourdet
Dr Georges Casalis
Francois Charbonnier
Jean-Pierre Faye

Georges Montaron
Robert Pontillon (International
   Secretary PSF)
Professor Albert Soboul

Germany
Ernst T. Bottcher
Dr Ingeborg Drewitz
Professor D.H. Gollwitzer
Michael Schwelien
Dr Hannes Schwenger
Professor Dr Ulrich Sonnemann
Professor Uwe Wesel

Greece
Panayiotis Canellakis
Manolis Glezos
Ilias Iliou
Stathis Panagoulis
Michel Raptis
Lefteris Apostolou
Lady Amalia Fleming

Holland
Professor Lolle Nauta

Hungary
Professor Andras Hegedus
Dr Agnes Heller
Ivan Szelenyi

Italy
Sen. Enzo Enriques Agnoletti
Sen. Lelio Basso
Giuseppe Boffa

Massimo Cacciari
Umberto Cerroni
Riccardo Lombardi
Giuliano Procacci
Paolo Spriano

Spain
Fernando Claudin

Norway
Professor Johan Galtung

Portugal
Otelo Saraiva de Carvalho

UK
Michael Barratt Brown
Howard Brenton
George Bridges
Norman Buchan, MP
Stuart Burge
Ken Coates
Mick Costello (National
    Industrial Organiser,
    Communist Party)
Geoff Edge, MP
Bob Edwards, MP
Chris Farley
Martin Flannery, MP
Ken Fleet
Trevor Griffiths
Mark Harrison
Eric S. Heffer, MP
Quintin Hoare *(New Left Review)*

Dr Stuart Holland
Martin Jacques *(Marxism Today)*
Monty Johnstone
Tom Litterick, MP
Professor Moshe Lewin
Joan Lestor, MP
Oscar Lewenstein
Dr Steven Lukes
Max Madden, MP
Joan Maynard, MP
Ian Mikardo, MP
Chris Myant
Stan Newens, MP˙
Denis Ogden
Tom Stoppard
Tony Topham
Audrey Wise, MP

USA
Professor Noam Chomsky
Stephen F. Cohen
Howard Fast
Joseph Hansen
Elizabeth Hardwick
Irving Howe
Corliss Lamont
Paul Sweezy

Yugoslavia
Professor Vladimir Dedijer
Dr Rudi Rizman

A Postscript
by Zhores Medvedev

In furtherance of the campaign reported above, the Russell Foundation sent a dossier on the response to Larin's appeal to a number of people. One of these was the distinguished Soviet biochemist, Zhores Medvedev. On the 18th July, just as this brochure was going to press, we received from him the following letter:

National Institute for Medical Research
London NW7 1AA
17th July 1978

Ken Coates,
Bertrand Russell Peace Foundation

Dear Ken

Thank you for sending me all your materials about Bukharin. As one of the authors of the book on *Khrushchev: The Years in Power,** I have, amongst our preparatory materials, some interesting information about the circumstances which prevented Khrushchev from securing official rehabilitation for Bukharin. Because we presented our book under a title limited to *The Years in Power* we were not able to use some interesting materials about Khrushchev's life after he was dismissed.

During the first years after his resignation (1965-1966) Khrushchev was in a state of depression, but later he resumed some activity, visited Moscow, and had visitors at his "dacha" where he lived and told them many of his memoirs. About 1968 Khrushchev was invited to see a play called *Bolsheviks* which was staged in the theatre "Sovre-

*This book, which was jointly written with Roy Medvedev, was published in 1977 by the Oxford University Press.

mennik" by the director and author of the play, M. Shatrov
— a man whom Khrushchev had known personally for a
long time. The play was about the events of 1918, the
attempted assassination of Lenin and the Bolsheviks'
reaction to this act. There was a scene of a meeting of
Bolshevik leaders, in which they discussed the events.
Khrushchev liked the play and after the performance he
visited the author and theatre director, M. Shatrov. During
a discussion at which some other members of the theatre
group were present, N. Khrushchev asked Shatrov: "You
reproduced the Party Central Committee meeting in 1918
— it was very convincing. But why were neither Kamenev,
nor Bukharin present? I know that they were in Moscow at
this time and took part in that meeting". Shatrov replied
that it was impossible to show either Bukharin, or Kamenev
or Trotsky because they had not been rehabilitated. Then
Khrushchev began to explain that Bukharin and Kamenev
were among the group of leaders whose rehabilitation was
under consideration in 1958 after the "elimination" of the
Molotov-Malenkov "anti-party" group from the Party
leadership.

The resolution about the reconsideration of the Moscow
show trials was already ready and it was decided to publish
it in newspapers. A Special Commission of the Central
Committee had already completed the work and recom-
mended rehabilitation. M. Suslov and some others were
against this rehabilitation, but the majority was in favour.
Probably Suslov alerted some of the leaders of the European Communist Parties. Among them, only the Italian
Party supported the whole process of rehabilitation and
wanted it to continue. Maurice Thorez, however, urgently
flew to Moscow and urged Khrushchev to postpone the
rehabilitation of Bukharin, Rykov, Zinoviev and others.
"After the XXth Congress and the Hungarian events we
lost almost half of our Party," said Thorez. "If you were
formally to rehabilitate these who were tried in the open
trials, we could loose the rest . . . You can rehabilitate
them later, not all at the same time, but one after another,
slowly". "These arguments influenced us", said Khrushchev,

"but I am now sorry that I followed this advice. We should have rehabilitated them, and we would certainly have done so, if not for the interference from Thorez".

The head of Khrushchev's guard (he was under 'protection' all the time after his dismissal), normally never interrupted Khrushchev's talks with other people. But at this meeting, he asked Khrushchev's wife (she was there) to take Khrushchev out as soon as possible.

Apart from this conversation, Khrushchev very often told visitors that he much regretted that during his time he stopped short of the rehabilitation of Bukharin and others.

This report was written from the evidence of those who were present at this talk and also from accounts by other visitors to Khrushchev and members of his large family.

All best wishes

Zhores Medvedev

Further Reading

For those who wish to know more about the life and work of Bukharin, it is necessary to read the important biography, by Stephen Cohen: *Bukharin and the Bolshevik Revolution*. Wildwood House, 1974. A bibliography of Bukharin's own writings was published by Sidney Heitman: *A Bibliography with Annotations*, Stanford University Press, California, 1967. Heitman also published a short essay in *Revisionism* (ed. Leopold Labedz), Allen and Unwin, 1962. Another short essay worth consulting is Alex Nove: *Some Observations on Bukharin and His Ideas*, in *Essays in Honour of E.H. Carr* (ed. Abramsky), MacMillan, 1974. Carr's own assessment of Bukharin is to be found in his preface to the Pelican Modern Classics edition of *The ABC of Communism*. Treatments of considerable interest are: Moshe Lewin: *Political Undercurrents in Soviet Economic Debates*, Pluto, 1975, and Boris Nicolaevksy: *Power and the Soviet Elite*, Ann Arbor, 1975.

*   *   *

For the background in Soviet political history, the indispensable work is: Roy Medvedev: *Let History Judge*, Spokesman 1976.

*   *   *

Concerning the trial, besides the works listed in footnotes above, notably that by Katkov, it will be instructive to read Arthur Koestler's *Darkness at Noon*, alongside Andy McSmith's *On a Point of History*, when this interesting modern treatment of the purges is published. The two volumes on the work of the Dewey Commission are still most helpful. Also, the writings of Trotsky himself on the Bukharin trial are still very much to the point. They are to be found in *Writings of Leon Trotsky, 1937-8*, Pathfinder, 1976.